362.2   Ryerson, Eric
RYE
         When your parent
         drinks too much

$14.95

DATE			
BR(8-2) Mar			

Self Help/Substance Abuse &
Addictions/Alcoholism

North Knox East
Junior High

When Your Parent Drinks Too Much

When Your Parent Drinks Too Much

A Book
for Teenagers

Eric Ryerson

Facts On File Publications
New York, New York ● Oxford, England

**When Your Parent Drinks Too Much
A Book for Teenagers**

Copyright © 1985 by Eric Ryerson

Library of Congress Cataloging in Publication Data

Ryerson, Eric.
    When your parent drinks too much.

    Summary: A self-help guide for teenagers with
alcoholic parents, discussing alcoholic parents,
discussing alcoholism, methods of dealing with it,
and where to go for help.
    1. Alcoholics—Family relationships—Juvenile
literature.   2. Children of alcoholic parents—Juvenile
literature. [1. Alcoholism.   2. Alcoholics]   I. Title.
HV5132.R94   1985   362.2'92   85-12961
ISBN 0-8160-1259-8

Printed in the United States of America
10   9   8   7   6   5

Composition by Facts On File/Circle Graphics
Printed by R.R. Donnelley & Sons Co.

For my mother,
for her love and her triumph,
one day at a time.

Contents

Acknowledgments

It may strike you as an author's cliche to say, "This book could not have been written without...". But it is a fact that the item in your hands would not be there were it not for the honesty and forthrightness of a number of bright, kind young people, who generously shared their thoughts and feelings about growing up with a parent who drinks too much. Talking to me was not easy for many of them—all the more reason why their contributions are so richly appreciated. They shall remain anonymous here (and their names have been changed in the text), not because they have anything to be ashamed of, but only in the interests of privacy—theirs as well as their alcoholic parent's. But they should know they've done a huge good deed by being so open, and that their sharing will help a lot of their peers who are feeling very confused and alone. To all of you, a heartfelt thanks.

Special thanks also are due Bill and Edith W., who gently showed me light and hope when I needed them most; Peggy M., a nurturing friend and all-around sage; the people

I've known and heard in Alateen and Al-Anon, for their sharing and caring; Gerry Helferich, my skillful editor, for his care and enthusiasm, and for knowing just when to prod; Ed W., a recovering alcoholic, for educating me about the disease and making sure I never miss anything written about it; Allison, a wise and loving sister, who knows a lot about recovery and has shared much of it with me; and especially to Denise, who, as ever, has been a well of love and kindness through this project—and a bottomless one at that.

Introduction:
You Are Not Alone

I am the child of an alcoholic. For 11 years I lived under the dark, horrible cloud of a parent's drinking problem. It was the most difficult time in my life, and looking back, it's not hard to see why: I was growing up in a place where all the things we need most from our families—love, support, stability—were washed away in a tidal wave of alcohol.

But back then I wasn't really aware of those larger issues. All I knew was that I lived with a daily dread—about how bad the drinking would be that day, about how much shouting, crying or fighting there might be and about when—or if—it was ever going to end. I never knew what to expect next. I lived with constant fear and worry. I felt ashamed and confused. But more than anything else, I felt alone.

I felt that way despite having a loving family—a father, brother, sister and grandmother—who all tried hard to help me and comfort me in their own ways; and despite having a lot of good friends, and seeming, on the outside, to have a lot going for me. But inside was a different story. Inside I felt isolated, even from my family. I felt different, even from my best friends. It was as though a black shadow hovered over our house, setting us apart from the other normal families. I was sure that none of my friends—really, no kid anywhere—had ever experienced the private hell and overwhelming hurt I was living through. And I was just as sure that nobody could ever understand.

Today my mother is sober. She has not had a drink in five years. I consider her recovery nothing less than a miracle, because for years I truly believed there would never be another sober moment in her life, or a sane and normal one in mine.

In this book you're going to learn a lot about the experiences and feelings I went through in the years of living with my alcoholic parent. You will also read about the experiences of a number of other people—most of them teenagers close in age to yourself—who have lived with the same problems, fears and worries.

Even if you've read just this far, chances are you either know or suspect that one of your parents has a problem with alcohol. Depending on how severe the problem is at this point, you're probably feeling a whole spectrum of different feelings, none of which is even remotely pleasant or comfortable. You may be confused, and why not? A big part of living with an alcoholic is living with uncertainty. Nothing is constant. Rules and messages are always changing. One day you may be allowed to stay out until 10 P.M., the next day you might get yelled at for not coming home right after school. One minute your drinking parent might order you to keep him* company, the next he might tell you to get out of his sight. Promises are made in bundles: "Tommorrow will be different;" "I'm only going to have two drinks tonight;" "We'll go to the amusement park on Saturday." More often

*For the sake of simplicity and clarity (and for no other reason) is the alcoholic referred to in this book in masculine gender: he, his, him. For the same reason, the non-drinking parent is identified with feminine pronouns. This should not be taken to mean that alcoholism is more a problem for men or women, or that if your mother is the problem drinker in your home, the difficulties you're facing are any different or less serious. While the particular troubles your family experiences may differ somewhat depending on whether it's your mother or father who has the drinking problem, the larger, underlying problems remain very much the same.

than not, they're broken.

You may also feel tense and afraid, never knowing what might happen next or what might trigger another disagreement or outburst. You're probably worried because nobody wants to talk about the drinking problem (silence is the watchword in most alcoholic families) and because you sense that nobody can do anything to make things better. You also probably feel angry and hurt about being mistreated and neglected, about how your needs and concerns have somehow gotten lost in the whole family's obsession with the bottle. I felt all these things at one time or another, and so did practically every young person I talked with. Plain and simple, it hurts to know that our parents aren't there for us.

Whatever your particular feelings, you can be sure that there are lots of others—literally millions of us—who have shared them. We understand what you're going through. This is a fact that you can count on, no matter how isolated and "different" you may feel, and it will become more and more evident as you continue reading. You're going to learn, as I did, that though every home situation has its own little twists and circumstances, the way that we, as children of alcoholics, respond to and feel about the problem is remarkably similar.

Knowing you have company out there is a vital first step in being able to let go of that gnawing, gut-wrenching sense of being different from every other kid on the planet, a feeling the disease drives into us with frightening force. Alcoholism, after all, is a terrifying thing. It is a wicked disease that we don't understand and can't control, and our fear makes us want to hide from it, cover it up and pretend it doesn't exist. It is often called a "disease of denial" for this very reason; even in the face of overwhelming evidence, everyone in the family—especially the alcoholic—tries hard to deny the problem exists. It hurts so much and causes so much inner turmoil to everyone in the home that our instinct is to recoil from it and suffer in silence. And the more we try to clamp a lid on all of our hurtful feelings, the harder we try to escape from the ugly reality of our home situation, the

more isolated we become from other people. Maggie, one of
the teenagers of an alcoholic I talked with, expressed it this
way:

> My mother's drinking got really bad when I was in
> eighth grade. I felt like one person out in the middle of
> the ocean. There was no one there. Nobody could
> understand, because I walled myself off from my friends
> and everyone else. I felt like I was in a little box. I felt like
> I was missing out on something because my best friends
> had great relationships with their mothers. And I was
> ashamed. I couldn't bring any friends over because the
> house was such a mess or because my mom would fall
> asleep in front of the television at 7 o'clock. And I'd have
> to make up some excuse like, "Oh, she's just so tired,"
> or "She's very comfortable in that chair." There were so
> many secrets. We were never allowed to talk about the
> drinking. My father exploded like a volcano if you tried
> to talk to him about Mom's drinking. I felt like nobody
> was there.

One of the most vivid memories of my childhood is of
walking up the block to my house after basketball practice.
Night is falling over the last flickers of daylight. Lights glow
in the windows of the big, comfortable homes, and the street
is quiet and serene, the only sound coming from the wintry
wind rustling the big old trees. Everything looks so tranquil
and orderly, and all the homes look the same, and I imagine
that inside the lighted windows everything is the same. Kids
are playing and dinner is cooking, everyone's getting ready
to sit down for the beginning of a relaxing family evening.
    Then I look at the lights in my house, and a cold
shudder goes through me. I feel sad because I know that
what's probably going on inside my house couldn't be
further from that soothing domestic scene. Who knows what
I'll find when I open the door? Who will be yelling at whom
this time? How far gone will my mom be? Will she be passed
out in her favorite drinking chair, or could this—please—be
a sober night for a change? Will she be nice or hostile? Will
Dad come home tonight? Will I be able to have any
semblance of peace? Or will it be another endless horror of

fighting, screaming and thuds in the middle of the night?

I don't know what I'll find. I never did. All I knew—or thought I knew—was that nobody had ever felt such hurt or shame or sadness. It all felt hopeless. I was sure the pain would never end and that it would be a miracle if I survived it.

But I was wrong. I learned not only that I wasn't alone, but also that the problem wasn't hopeless. I learned I could make changes that would make me happier and make my life better, even if I couldn't control the drinking problem. Those changes and the ways I found to pick up the pieces of a life that often felt too shattered to ever put back together is what we're going to be talking about through the rest of the book.

I think you'll find help and hope in the pages that follow. I also think you'll find comfort and wisdom—qualities that spring directly from the good, kind people who have shared what you're going through and who have donated their honesty, insights and sensitivity to this book's cause.

Even now as an adult, I'm steadily gaining a better understanding of how growing up with an alcoholic parent has shaped and affected my life. Working on this book has greatly aided that process. It has given me a chance to listen to and share experiences with many other people, and it has enhanced my understanding of the ways we can work on ourselves and the actions we can take to make our lives better. If the reading is anywhere near as uplifting for you as the writing has been for me, the book's mission will have been richly accomplished.

When Your Parent Drinks
Too Much

Some Facts about Alcoholism | 1

We're all affected by our environments; there's no way around it. Responding to the circumstances we find ourselves in is as basic as breathing and eating. If you're surrounded by a horde of smokers, you're going to inhale smoke whether you like it or not. When more people in your classroom are sneezing and coughing than taking notes, you're going to be engulfed by germs and at high risk for catching a bug.

The moods and attitudes of the people we're around can affect us in the same way. If you're with people who are laughing and singing, it's not hard for the feeling to rub off on you. By the same token, if gloom and doom are the outlook you're picking up, that can seep into you just as easily.

The point is that none of us is an island. So it's not surprising that living with a parent who has a drinking problem has a profound impact on us. Alcoholism can inflict damage on anyone who has regular, close contact with the alcoholic. We don't catch the disease the way we catch a cold, from exposure to germs, but we catch it just the same—from being around people we love very much who have slipped into unhealthy attitudes and destructive behavior.

But the damage we suffer doesn't have to be extreme, and it certainly isn't irreversible. There are definite actions and attitudes that can limit the disease's impact on us and help us do constructive things for ourselves in spite of the major problems brought on by living with an alcoholic parent. The first step toward that end is to learn more about the drinking problem itself, and how and why alcohol can seize control and enslave a person to its intoxicating effects.

WHAT IS ALCOHOLISM?

Alcoholism is a disease characterized by a compulsion to drink. Alcoholics are people who cannot control their drinking and whose drinking interferes with their day-to-day lives, provoking problems and conflicts that get worse as time goes on. The problems at the beginning may seem small and of no special concern. Maybe your parent will fall asleep on the sofa after having a "nightcap" or two. Maybe he'll begin coming home later because he likes to stop off at a bar to "unwind" from a hard day. Or perhaps you'll notice that cocktail time seems to be starting earlier, or that your parents are arguing more than they used to, or that your parent is more unpredictable than before, barking at you over a small issue and letting a larger one just slide by. None of these situations is particularly alarming. Nor does their occurrence mean that a person definitely is an alcoholic.

What's important to keep in mind is that a drinking problem can be subtle at the beginning, but in time (maybe in a few months, maybe in a few years—there's no precise timetable) the disease will get worse and worse. Before the alcoholic may have come home late; now he may not come home at all. The unpleasant shouting matches your parents used to have were bad enough; suddenly they've escalated to night-long battles that might include cursing, throwing things and even physical abuse. What was moodiness before may now appear to be full-blown Jekyll and Hyde behavior by the problem drinker. This steady deterioration is why alcoholism is called a progressive disease, and why it can lead to increasingly serious complications, even death or insanity, if it goes unchecked. It does not go away or get cured the way other diseases can; the alcoholic's inability to control his drinking always stays with him. But while the disease itself can't be cured, it can be halted, and it can be recovered from. Most professionals in the field agree that the only way recovery can occur is if the alcoholic abstains from alcohol completely. They talk about "crossing the line" from drinking socially to drinking alcoholically. Once the line is crossed, the alcoholic cannot go back to light or moderate drinking—the way the person may have started drinking in the first place. As sure as I'm writing and you're reading, the alcoholic will try to convince you that he *can* still control his drinking, that he can roll his habit back to his more moderate levels of last month or last year. But as desperately as he wants to convince you—and himself—that he still has the upper hand over his compulsion, he doesn't. It's out of his control.

HOW CAN YOU TELL IF YOUR PARENT IS AN ALCOHOLIC?

Some people think that to be an alcoholic you have to be a skid-row bum. But this is an old and mistaken notion. The fact is, only three percent of all alcoholics are skid-row types; the rest are made up of people of all races, religions, ethnic origins and income groups. The only prerequisite to being an alcoholic is to be addicted to the drug alcohol.

Determining if a person is an alcoholic* is far from an exact science. Problem drinkers can behave very differently. Some may drink wine, others beer, while others may prefer hard liquor, such as vodka, gin or scotch; what one drinks

*The terms "alcoholic" and "problem drinker" are used interchangeably in this book.

has no bearing on whether a person is an alcoholic. Nor does the quantity or frequency of the drinking necessarily give you a clue; some problem drinkers will drink themselves into a stupor every night, yet others may just have a few drinks at the outset, and may even decide to stop drinking altogether for a day, a week, maybe even a month or more (usually to prove to the family that they can control the drinking).

There were plenty of times when I thought the problem was over because my mom temporarily went on the wagon. Sometimes the dry spell would last two or three weeks. My hopes soared sky-high with every moment of temporary tranquility, but they only came crashing back to earth when the drinking resumed, as it always did, because the disease was alive and kicking—all of us.

So how can you tell if your parent has a drinking problem? Practically speaking, a problem almost certainly exists if your parent's drinking interferes with some facet of the family life. Maybe relationships become strained when your parent is drinking. (Is that when you get yelled at about your grades or your messy room? Is that when you never know what to expect?) Maybe your parent is having job problems. (Has he ever called in sick after a hard night of drinking? Does he report to work late, talk about his three-martini lunches, or about how the boss has it in for him?) Maybe family plans and schedules are constantly getting fouled up. (Are dinners put off for an hour or two so there's time for a few more drinks? Did you miss out on the ball game or concert because your parent made other plans because he didn't remember?) Or maybe there's just a lot more fighting around the house, as the alcoholic points fingers at how everyone else is making a mess of family life. (Does the problem drinker complain about being unappreciated, a slave for everyone else, about how pressures at work or the behavior of the rest of the family are driving him to drink?) The list is endless.

Several key symptoms provide other ways of determining if a drinking problem exists. A distinct personality change while under the influence of alcohol is one reliable indicator. Perhaps your drinking parent, normally a calm person, becomes loud and hostile when drinking. Another trouble sign is when a parent suffers from a blackout, which occurs when a drinker, though remaining conscious, "blacks out" and forgets what happened for a period of time. Perhaps the most telltale sign of all is when there are signs of progression.

Maybe your parent is showing less and less control over his drinking, getting intoxicated more often and seeming unable to stop once he starts. Maybe he is becoming less dependable, and his behavior while drinking more unpredictable. Perhaps you're seeing that alcohol is taking center stage in your parent's life, and that he's increasingly unavailable to you. When this occurs, his disease has progressed to the point where if he isn't already drunk, he's thinking about how and when he's going to be. He literally becomes a slave to his need to drink, and the ever-worsening addiction leaves little room for you, your other parent or any of the other important people in the alcoholic's life.

Inevitably, problems mount as the drinking gets worse. Bills go unpaid. The drinker's job, if not lost, may be in jeopardy. Chores and projects around the home remain undone, and family plans and outings are pushed aside. The long-promised shopping trip? Some other time. The help with your special school project? Now isn't convenient. The weekend visit to Grandma and Grandpa? Well, the alcoholic may get you there, but maybe you wished he hadn't; he's got a drink in his hand all weekend, and all you can think about is how loaded he's going to get—and how much you hate his drinking. As the disease progresses the family (as we'll discuss in more detail later) probably will become much more active in covering up the problem. Got a friend coming over? Better make it another time, or better yet, convince your friend that you should meet at his house instead. Did the neighbors see the drinker fall flat on his face on the front porch? Oh, well, he just tripped on a bad step. Scared by a disease we don't understand, our instinct is to hide it—from others, and even from ourselves.

A DISEASE OF DENIAL

Even as things get worse, the alcoholic typically will deny that any problem exists. In fact, he will likely become very angry at the slightest hint by you or someone else that alcohol is causing difficulties. My mother would fly into a rage at the mere mention of the word "alcoholic." As far as she was concerned, it was the dirtiest word in the English language.

Deep down, the problem drinker knows there's trouble, but his denial remains fierce. Desperately afraid of having to face the truth and give up drinking, alcoholics are great at deluding themselves into thinking the problem doesn't exist. Perhaps you recognize some of these excuses, which I heard in my home for years:

- I don't have a drinking problem. I have other problems, and the drinking is just a symptom.
- I can stop anytime I want to.
- I'm just going through a hard time. Why can't you show me some sympathy instead of getting on my case about having a drink to relax?
- Everybody drinks. It's not my fault our friends are all teetotalers.
- If you were in my shoes, you'd drink too.

You may feel hurt, angry and deeply frustrated if your parent is denying the problem. For a long time, I felt like screaming from the hilltops, "Can't you see what you're doing? If you don't care about yourself, what about me? How can you say there's not a problem? Why don't you look in the mirror, or at the broken lamp you tripped over last night, or think about the neighbor you yelled at because she didn't want you to come over for cocktails?" I thought if I showed her the evidence or got upset enough, my mother might be moved to see there really was a problem. Unfortunately, that isn't the way it works. The denial is deeply entrenched, and the only way it's overcome is when the alcoholic gets so low and is swamped by so many problems that the wall of denial is crumbled by the sad weight of the truth.

It's very painful to see a parent, someone we look to for direction and support, ignoring the truth so totally. It helps to keep in mind that it's a part of the disease—one that everyone who has lived with alcoholism has butted his head against. In later chapters we'll look at things you can do to help your parent confront the reality of the problem—and decide to take steps to overcome it.

WHY ALCOHOLICS DRINK

Think for a moment of a few things you don't like. A particular vegetable, a dumb television show, the kid down the block who talks about you behind your back—there are probably lots of things you could do without. Whatever it is, you instinctively try to avoid it as much as you can. It's perfectly natural; if something or someone causes you discomfort, you stay away.

For the problem drinker alcohol is a way to avoid things. It's an escape, a crutch he can use to prop himself up when he feels weighed down with problems and worries. Alcohol seems to make life easier to face. It helps the drinker relax and eases the knot he might feel in his stomach. It soothes his worry and helps him forget about how lonely or depressed he is, or about how little he thinks of himself. It makes his problems go away, at least temporarily. Plenty of people who are so-called social drinkers have a drink or two because it helps them relax, but the difference is that they retain control over their drinking. They don't cross that line. For them, alcohol brings on a pleasant, soothing sensation; their drinking has nothing to do with fleeing from internal pressures.

The problem drinker, on the other hand, gradually loses control over alcohol. He gets into the habit of turning to alcohol to soften life's rough edges and develops an emotional dependence on it. Alcohol becomes the way out. It provides relief, and for the alcoholic that feeling is far more comfortable than getting overwhelmed by his problems. He gets hooked on the pain-numbing quality of alcohol, becoming increasingly unable to cope with life in any way other than the bottle. Eventually, this powerful psychological addiction gives way to physical addiction—a point when the alcoholic experiences withdrawal symptoms such as shakiness, headaches, nausea and even hallucinations if he goes without alcohol for too long.

Despite years of scientific study, we still don't know precisely what makes a person become an alcoholic. What is it that allows some people to stay in control of their drinking and others to lose it totally? Theories abound. Some experts think it may be a genetic factor—an actual physiological condition that is coded into us along with our eye color and body type. One reason for the heredity theory is that alcoholism is a disease that runs in families. In fact, we children of alcoholics, studies show, are approximately four times as likely to become problem drinkers ourselves as those who did not grow up with the problem.

Other professionals in the field, however, lean to the learned-response theory of alcoholism, saying that the reason the disease tends to be passed on in families is because kids, over time, acquire the same difficulties dealing with problems that their role models—their parent or parents—have.

We're probably a ways off from understanding the exact origins of alcoholism. But whatever its causes, the central point is that problem drinkers have trouble coping with their lives and turn to alcohol for help. Long before the problem drinker is aware of it, alcohol becomes his much-needed escape hatch from the pressures, doubts and worries that are churning inside him—a hatch he turns to more and more as the disease progresses.

A PARTING THOUGHT

As you watch alcoholism take hold, you may feel as though your parent has practically become possessed by some demonic force, that evil has swooped in and taken over, leaving nothing of your parent's former self. In a sense, that *is* what's going on. The person my mother became under the influence of alcohol bore no resemblance to the kind, loving person I'd known my whole life. She was riddled with the disease. She was belligerent, angry, manipulative and inconsiderate, and everything in her life, including me, took a back seat to her compulsion to drink.

Seeing her that way flooded me with painful feelings. I felt sad, angry, ashamed, rejected, confused and frustrated—sometimes, it seemed, all at once. Gradually, with a little time and the kindness and support of others who shared my problem, things got better for me, just as they can get better for you.

This is not blind, naive optimism. Do you feel the situation with your parent is hopeless? So did I. Do you think sometimes that the problem will never end? So did I. Are there times when you feel like giving up or running away and hiding, and never laying eyes on the alcoholic again? I've felt those things, too. But these feelings and everything else that's inside us can be eased and mended. A healing process can begin, and you can clear yourself a path that's a healthier and much more positive course for your life. *Where* it begins is with the knowledge of what we discussed in this chapter: that your parent has a disease and even as he (and probably everyone else) tries to deny it, the problem is steadily getting worse and is inflicting serious pain and damage to all those exposed to it. Now let's see how this knowledge can relieve some of your burden and make feeling better more than a far-off dream.

The Three C's|2

I was plenty skeptical when I first heard talk—at age 14—of alcoholism being a disease. "What's it got to do with disease?" I asked myself. "My mother drinks too much. If she'd stop it, everything would be fine."

But she could not stop—not by herself, not without support and treatment—and that's precisely why it is a disease. Heart disease is characterized by a narrowing of the blood vessels. Diabetes is characterized by an inability to produce insulin. Alcoholism is characterized by a compulsion to drink.

The American Medical Association recognizes alcoholism as a disease. So does the World Health Organization. So have a lot of other authorities, and for a long time. In the 19th century, a physician named Benjamin Rush took note of how chronic drinking "resembles certain hereditary, family and contagious diseases." Even the ancient Roman philosopher Seneca, writing in the first century, distinguished between "a man who is drunk" and one who "has no control over himself...who is a slave to the habit."

WHY THE DISEASE CONCEPT IS SO IMPORTANT

If you've talked over your family problems with someone such as a counselor or a trusted friend, perhaps you fully accept that your parent is suffering from a disease. Or maybe you share my first reaction and feel the idea makes little sense of the situation. But no matter whether the notion of alcoholism as a disease is new or troublesome (right now) for you, I can tell you that it's the best ally you have for coping effectively with your parent's drinking problem. It's the critical starting point for feeling better, because, among other things, it makes clear that the drinking problem is not something you should take personally.

Your parent is not drinking too much because he doesn't care for you. Nor is he willfully trying to hurt you. It almost certainly feels that way to you sometimes, as it did to me, particularly when the drunken scenes were hostile and embarrassing. I remember one time when I was playing ball in my backyard with a friend. My mom came to the door, obviously in bad shape, and ordered me to come into the house to keep her company. I was terrified she might act up. The last thing I wanted was a shouting match. I answered politely: "Please let me finish our game, okay? Then I'll be right in." She disappeared and I breathed a sigh of relief.

Maybe my friend didn't notice how she slurred her words, I thought. Maybe he won't find out my mom is a drunk. We resumed playing. Minutes later she reappeared at the door. My heart sank. "Get in here now, dammit," she screamed. "Tell Bob [my friend] to go home because you've got to take care of your drunken mother."

I was mortified. "I guess I better go," said my friend awkwardly. How could she do this to me? I wanted to know. How could she humiliate me in front of my friend? Doesn't she know how this makes me feel?

I was taking it personally because I hadn't yet accepted

that my mother was riddled with a horrible disease that could make her behave in repulsive ways. Practically all of us have trouble with this concept at first. Listen to Maggie talk about her feelings about her alcoholic mother:

> We'd fight all the time when she was drinking. She'd fall asleep in the chair every night and the drink would spill all over. It was scary. I never knew what to do. Whenever I'd get upset and cry, she'd ship me off to a psychiatrist and tell me I was a problem child. I really started to hate her. I said "I hate you" to her more times than I can count, and it was because of her drinking. I always wondered, "When will she realize what she's doing to me?"

Failing to realize that alcoholism is a disease tends to make us blame the drinker for his condition. I sometimes would treat my mother as though she were a naughty child, scolding her for her bad habit. But no matter how bad the situation is, we have no right to do that. Blaming someone assumes he is at fault, and alcoholism has nothing to do with being at fault. Alcoholics do not drink because they're bad people. They drink because they have a disease that unleashes an uncontrollable craving for alcohol. Sometimes when I've been having trouble with the disease concept, it has helped me to ask myself, "Would I blame my mother if her body couldn't manufacture enough insulin because she had diabetes? Would I blame her if she was prone to seizures because she had epilepsy?" These questions help remind me that a drinking problem, like any illness, has nothing to do with a person's moral failings.

LIGHTENING YOUR BURDEN

Acknowledging alcoholism as a disease not only saves us from pointing a finger at our parents, it also saves us from pointing a finger at ourselves. One thing I'm always struck by in talking to young people who have lived with a drinking problem is how many of them think deep down that somehow they were the cause of their parent's drinking. Maybe Dad gets upset when you bring home a crummy report card and decides to quell his anger with a double martini. Maybe Mom flies into such a rage because you still haven't done your chores that she turns to wine to calm her frayed nerves.

But remember, this is a disease we're talking about. You didn't cause it anymore than you can cause your parent to acquire some other sickness. Nor can you control it or cure it; your parent's drinking is altogether beyond your power. Taken together, these facts sometimes are called the three C's: You didn't cause your parent's drinking. You can't control it. And you can't cure it. Planting these concepts into your mind will do a lot to clear your head and ease some of the load you're carrying around. Let's look at them more closely.

YOU DIDN'T CAUSE YOUR PARENT'S DRINKING

We've looked at how problem drinkers typically go to great lengths to deny that the problem exists. One of the ways they do it is by insisting that excessive drinking isn't their problem, but rather the symptom of other problems. Usually "the other problems" means his spouse and/or kids. Often you'll hear alcoholics say things like, "You'd drink too if you had a wife like mine," or "My kids are driving me to drink," or maybe, "I'm a nervous wreck with all these family problems. So what's wrong with taking a drink to calm my anxiety?"

Sometimes the alcoholic won't blame you so explicitly. He may talk more generally about pressures, worries, how things are getting to him, rather than come right out and accuse you of making him fix himself a gin and tonic. Said Maggie:

My mom never specifically blamed me. But she would always say things like, "Nobody treats me right or thinks about me. Everyone thinks I'm the maid around here." It was a martyr routine. She'd complain that everyone was against her and she had to do everything—clean and cook and chauffeur people around. But since I was the youngest, and the one who needed to be driven and cooked for, it was pretty clear to me that when she said everyone she really meant me.

Whether the blame is direct or indirect, the message we children get is that we're the ones who are responsible for the problem, and that if we were somehow better—better students, more obedient, neater, more reliable or trustworthy, nicer to our brothers and sisters—that the drinking problem would magically disappear or at the very least greatly diminish.

But we have to keep telling ourselves that this simply isn't so. Forgetting to mow the lawn and having your father get angry is not causing him to be an alcoholic. Nor is the fight you had with your little brother. A disease is not brought on by such things, and the more you can keep that in mind—particularly when the blame is flying in your direction—the better you're going to feel.

Remember, part of the alcoholic's disease is to find someone to blame for all of his problems. After all, he can't blame the person who is responsible—himself—because to do that would be to admit that serious trouble exists, a truth he desperately wants to avoid. So he points fingers all around the house, and chances are he does so loudly and emphatically. His illness really wants him to make you—and himself—believe that everyone and everything but himself is the root of the problem. Although you probably wouldn't lay claim to being a model youth, having shortcomings, no matter what they may be, has nothing to do with making your parent abuse alcohol.

YOU CAN'T CONTROL YOUR PARENT'S PROBLEM

I could fill the rest of this book with tales of how I tried to control my mother's drinking. Hiding bottles, pouring them out, diluting drinks with soda and ice, switching soda for alcohol—I tried it all. I also tried pleading and begging, hoping it might yield a promise to take the night off from the bottle (a futile effort in any case, since even the most solemn vows are broken by problem drinkers). When all those things failed, as they always did, I'd bring out the heavy artillery: guilt. "You wouldn't drink if you loved me," I'd say, often at ear-splitting levels. "If you really cared, you'd stay sober tonight." That didn't work either, and for a long while I thought it really was because my mother didn't love me, or at least not the way she used to.

Eventually I came to see that it was a mistake to think anything I did could control my mom's drinking. Gradually I accepted that her drinking had nothing whatever to do with her feelings about me or anyone else. She was sick with a compulsion to drink. She was powerless over her drinking. So was I.

It's entirely understandable to want to stop your parent from drinking. After all, the stuff is wreaking all kinds of destruction in your family life. Just about everyone I talked with in writing this book spent vast amounts of time and energy attempting to control their alcoholic's drinking. At age seven, Diane would follow her father to bars, hoping to talk him out of going inside. John would retreat to his room and ignore his mother, trying to use silent scorn to get her to change her drunken ways. Francis related the time he woke up to the harsh sound of hammering—his dad nailing shut the liquor cabinet so his mom couldn't get at it. Elise may have had the most creative approach of all: she and her brother would move the clock ahead and go to their bedrooms, pretending they were asleep, so their mom would think it was bedtime, finish her drink and hit the sack. Then Elise and her brother would get up again—and hope their mom wouldn't.

Sometimes it's true that for a night or two you can curtail the drinking. Maybe you'll hide the supply and the liquor stores will be closed. Maybe you can drive off in the car or hide your parent's wallet, so he's got no means to get more.

But even if stunts such as these work in the short run, it's very important to see that ultimately they will do no good at all. Francis said the house was quiet for a few days after the cabinet had been nailed shut, but then his mother devised ways to get more liquor. Diane's tagging along may have slowed down her father from time to time, but he got to the bar just the same. My pleading would occasionally result in my mother announcing she would have just two or three drinks that night, but even if she kept her word, the next day things would revert right back to the same sadly familiar pattern.

Letting Go of the Urge to Control

Human beings like to control things. It's part of our nature. We want to feel we can have an impact on a situation—take an action and have it make a difference—and it's highly frustrating when we can't.

It's up to us to face the fact that someone else's drinking is one of those things we *can't* control. Trying to do so is not only useless—we might as well spend our time knocking our heads against the wall—it also can cause a lot of hurt and damage inside us.

This may not make sense to you on the face of it; it didn't to me when I first heard it. "How can trying to stop my mom from getting smashed do anything to me?" I thought to myself. "I'm only trying to help her, help me, help the whole family. What harm can that cause?"

A lot, for a couple of reasons. One is that the harder you try to control something that you can't control, the more open you are to a gnawing, frustrating sense of helplessness. Nothing you do is going to work, and that'll take you to the end of your rope in a hurry. The other reason is that the net effect of your earnest effort is to make you feel like a failure. You pour all this energy into trying to stop the drinking and it doesn't change a thing; how else can that make you feel? I wanted to stop my mother's drinking more than anything in the world, and as I said, I tried every approach I could think of. Over time my repeated failures took their toll on me. I wasn't conscious of feeling like a failure, but that was the self-image that was seeping in because I *had* failed. There wasn't a shred of anything to show for my efforts. I felt like a screw-up. And it wasn't until I really worked at accepting the alcoholism as a disease completely beyond my control that the burden of failure began to lift.

I emphasize the idea of working to accept your lack of control. It is work; it's not easy to convince yourself that you are powerless over something that's so tangible and painful and happening right before you. I just had to keep saying, almost as if it were a chant: "My mother has a disease, and I can't control it."

YOU CAN'T CURE YOUR PARENT'S DISEASE

Even after they accept that their parent has an illness, some people still expect themselves to make that illness go away. "I kind of felt that I should be nicer to my dad and he wouldn't have to drink as much," said James.

"I figured if I helped solve my mom's problems, she would have less to escape from," said Jeanine.

"I was my mother's favorite," added Maggie, "and our special bond made me feel a big burden that I should be able to help her get rid of her problem." I, too, thought my behavior could help provide a cure for alcoholism. Many nights I stayed home when my mother complained of being lonely hoping the company would show her that she didn't need to drink and that things could be just like always. I wanted desperately to rid her of the compulsion to drink, and if self-sacrifice was what it would take, it was okay by me.

But neither self-sacrifice nor anything else can cure a person of alcoholism. You can't "love" it out of someone and you can't make it go away by being neater, more dependable, a better student or hanging up your wet towels. There are attitudes and ways of behaving that can create an atmosphere around the home which can help your alcoholic parent face his problem, and we'll look closely at those things shortly. But for now the key point is that your parent's disease is beyond your power to cure. You can't make him want to give up drinking. You can't use reason or logic to highlight the harm he's doing to himself. You can't try to force him to see—as I often did—that he's drinking himself into a deeper and deeper mess. An alcoholic cannot and will not stop drinking until he wants to, until he can no longer hide from the damage alcohol is inflicting on himself and his loved ones, and wants to get help of his own free will.

SUMMING UP

Alcoholism is a disease that we did not cause, can't control and can't cure. Our parent is not at fault for having the disease, and we're certainly not at fault either. The drinking parent's denial often prompts him to blame and accuse us for causing his woes, but we have to bear in mind that he's singling us out only because part of his disease is to deny the sad reality of his deteriorating life.

We also must resist engaging in tricks and traps to keep the drinker away from drink. It may work temporarily, but over the long haul everybody loses. We have no power over the alcoholic's compulsion for drinking; he will always find a way to get more—until he decides that he cannot allow his life to continue its downward spiral any longer.

We must work at stamping these realizations about the Three C's into our consciousness. Because the more we're able to do it, the more we'll let go of the natural impulse to make our alcoholic parent see the light and make the drinking go away, the more energy and clarity we'll have to do things that really can make a positive difference in our lives.

The Family Disease|3

Alcoholism runs in families. Study after study has shown how the majority of alcoholics come from families in which one or more members—parent, grandparent, sibling, even an aunt or uncle—have or have had a drinking problem. Studies also show that children of alcoholics are at an especially high risk of developing a drinking problem, as we've noted.

This does not mean we're doomed. Nor does it mean, when it's time to decide about our own use of alcohol, that we must vow never to let the stuff touch our lips. But it does mean we need to be careful because the facts show that even though it hasn't been proved that the disease is actually inherited—passed on in the genes—it has been proved that certain families are predisposed to alcohol abuse, much as some families are predisposed to heart disease or diabetes.

WHY "THE FAMILY DISEASE"?

It would seem logical that the term "family disease" stems from this tendency, but there's an even more basic reason alcoholism is described that way. And it's because unlike most other illnesses which afflict only the person who suffers from it, alcoholism gradually works its way into everyone who's exposed to it for any length of time. We begin suffering the affects of the disease as well, not by acquiring a compulsion to drink, but by unconsciously falling into twisted thinking, negative attitudes and unhealthy behavior. This does not happen to some of us who live with alcoholism; it happens to *all* of us. A drinking problem would be far easier to cope with—and a book such as this wouldn't be necessary—if the trouble were limited to the excessive consumption of alcohol. But alcoholism is also a disease of relationships, an illness whose deep psychological roots reach into the family, with negative consequences for everyone. Understanding how we become infected by the disease that's all around us is important to our ability to deal with it in a healthier way and to make constructive changes in our lives.

PHYSICAL EFFECTS

Sometimes we suffer actual physical symptoms from the tension and anxiety that are rife in alcoholic homes. Have you had more trouble sleeping since the drinking became worse? Been awakened by recurring nightmares? Suffered from signs of nervousness, such as a twitch or shaky hands? Felt a knot in your stomach that practically never goes away? None of these reactions is in the least unusual. There's no reason to feel afraid or messed up because your body may be reacting to the tremendous stress you're living with. The truth is, most of us develop one physical side-effect or another. Carolyn suffered not only from terrible nightmares, but also from bouts of periodic bed-wetting. I went through a period where my hands shook uncontrollably whenever I needed them to be steady. I remember playing pool in my friend's basement, and drawing back the cue stick and not being able to strike the ball squarely because my hands wouldn't stay still. My friends joked about it and I tried to laugh it off, but I was embarrassed. I didn't know what was causing it. I hated it. It scared me because it seemed beyond my control.

Maggie had a more serious ailment, missing an entire semester of school with severe stomach pains. In the beginning she says she staunchly denied any connection betweeen her illness and the drinking, because that would be saying it was a psychosomatic problem, a pain that was caused by her head. But with the help of therapy she came to see how her parent's drinking and her very real pain had become linked. "I think it's how I showed the neglect," Maggie said. "I would keep getting sick and that way my mom would *have* to take care of me. Being sick was how you got attention in my family. One of my parents would stay by your bed at night and bring you soup and soda and change the channel on the TV. I was sick for about five months. It was the only way I could get love or attention. I just felt like I didn't have a mother, or that she was off in her own world. And my father worked and traveled at lot, and he'd usually get home late and barely talk to me."

HAVING DIFFICULTY CONCENTRATING

Bill is one of my best and oldest friends. He's also one of the smartest people around. But you never would've known that if you'd seen him in sixth grade.

Bill grew up with an alcoholic father. His dad finally got sober, and as Bill advanced to junior high and high school, the family recovered from the disease and their home became a very happy one. But for a long time it was anything but that, and Bill showed a number of effects from it, the foremost being his performance in school. He got poor grades, could never remember his homework and was aloof and inattentive in class. Teachers yelled at him all the time.

He was shifted from class to class because his teachers thought he couldn't keep up with the others. How surprised those teachers would be if they could see where Bill is today—a prominent young doctor who graduated from one of the top medical schools in the country.

Bill's childhood difficulties are far from unique to those who grow up as we do. He could never seem to keep focused. His mind wandered in class and he often seemed as though he were only half there.

The ability to concentrate is something a lot of people take for granted. But many of us don't have that luxury. Our thoughts are constantly shifting back to the trouble at home, and we become filled with worries about how bad things are and how much worse they might get. Dread can become our constant companion. Even when we're not actually in the alcoholic environment, we can have a hard time escaping the confusion and discord that are such a big part of it. With all these feelings swirling about in our troubled heads, is it any wonder that it's hard for us to concentrate or think as clearly as we want?

AN OBSESSION WITH ALCOHOL

As we continue living with the problem drinker, a gradual and damaging process unfolds: We begin to become as obsessed with alcohol as the alcoholic. Frequently without realizing it, we devote an increasing chunk of our time to thoughts and actions concerning drinking. We engage in a grim, destructive game with the alcoholic, where he finds all kinds of ways to drink and we find just as many to stop him. It's a game in which everybody loses—the alcoholic because the progression of the disease makes him worse and worse, and us because we feel growing frustration, helplessness and despair over our failure to "fix" him.

We've talked about how we can't control the drinking. But when we become thoroughly preoccupied with the alcoholism, we often slip into controlling ways, whether we know better or not. You might try asking yourself these questions, which will give you insights into how wrapped up you are in the bottle:

- Even when you're not with the alcoholic, do your thoughts often drift to the drinking, and to projecting about what condition he'll be in the next time you see him?
- Do you keep track of how much he's drinking, either by counting drinks or by drawing lines on the bottle?
- Do you ever search the house for bottles he may have hidden?
- Have you ever tried to hide the liquor or pour it down the drain?
- Do you dilute his drinks, or try to convince him to drink beer or wine so he won't get as drunk?
- Do you give him dirty looks, the cold shoulder or make a cutting remark ("I can't believe you're still thirsty after last night") when you see he's drinking, or even beginning to?

For me every answer is "yes." I was too close to the situation, too consumed by worry and confusion, to see the extent of my preoccupation at the time. But now I realize that as the problem got worse in my home, a vast amount of my time and energy was turned over to a constant alcohol vigil. And the same holds true for everyone else in the family as well. Alcohol took center stage in our home life. We'd hunt for bottles together, check liquor levels together and often shame the alcoholic together, in vain hopes of making her feel so guilty she would stop drinking. "Look at what you're doing to us;" "Look at what a pigsty the house is;" "Why did you drink tonight when you promised to be sober?"—these were the sorts of guilt-bearing arrows we would pierce her with, as if she were simply being naughty and as if her excessive drinking were solely a failure of willpower. We meant well; all we wanted was for the problem drinking to end and for things to be the way they had been. But pouring liquor down drains, hiding bottles and peddling guilt have never and will never take care of a drinking problem. In our obsession, what we failed to realize—and what most of us fail to realize when things begin to get bad—is the most essential understanding of all, namely that we are up against a disease that we have no power over. Again and again, we tried applying external controls—measures that were doomed to failure and whose only impact was to make us feel increasingly frustrated, angry and like failures ourselves—for not being able to do anything about the problem.

Maybe as you mull over this obsession business, you're thinking, "How can you not think a lot about the drinking? It's not like it's easy to overlook." Well, I agree, it's not a problem that's easily ignored. But what we're talking about is a question of degree. Of course it's impossible to not think at all about the drinking, to not spend some time worrying about whether he's at the bottle when we're away. But as we're exposed more and more to the drinking, most of us lose some of our mental balance. Our thinking becomes distorted and we begin fighting harder and harder to stop the alcoholic from getting at the stuff. We become more grimly determined to save him and ourselves. Our mental wheels whir constantly as we concoct clever new ways to solve the whole mess. We become, in a word, obsessed. And it harms us not only because the efforts are destined to fail, but also because slowly but surely a host of other, healthier activities drop out of the picture. We have less time for our friends. We stop looking out for ourselves. We have less time for fun. And even when we do try to get away from the hurt, we have a harder time succeeding at it because part of our minds remain locked into the woes at home.

THE WALL OF ISOLATION

If there's one thing we in alcoholic families are good at, it's keeping secrets. We're too good at it, in fact, and the result is that we conceal so much of our true selves, our innermost thoughts and feelings, that we become withdrawn and isolated from other people.

Our biggest secret, of course, is the drinking itself. Afraid and confused by its ugly intrusion, most of us deal with it by running for cover. We feel ashamed about it (at least we do until we accept that alcoholism is a disease that has nothing to do with the drinker being a bad person) and think it's a bad reflection on us, so our impulse is to go to almost any length to hide it from friends, neighbors and others outside the family. We gradually close ourselves off. We arrange that our friends come over to our houses as infrequently as possible. We make up lies to keep them away and if they do happen to see our parent drunk, we make up lies to try to cover up the drinking. "Oh, he wasn't slurring his words, he was just really tired from a hard day," we might say. Or if someone asks, "What's wrong with your mom?" we might come up with a terse "nothing" and hope the subject is dropped. "Sometimes my friends ask me questions about my mother," related Timothy. "I always get right off the subject. I get tight inside when they press the issue. I'll deny what's going on or that anything is wrong. If they keep pressing I'll just leave." Such situations became so uncomfortable for Timothy that he began seeing his friends less and less. "I'd get home from school, go to my room and close the door, put on records and stay there for hours, just thinking. I retreated pretty severely. It's weird about the isolation. I don't know what did it to me. But I didn't go anywhere. I became a hermit."

I did much the same thing. My room was my refuge. It was about the only place that felt safe. It was where I could be alone with my secrets. I wasn't having what you'd call a good time in there, but that's another way the disease affects us: Many of us don't care about having a good time. All we want is to not have a bad time, to not feel any more painful feelings than we're already feeling. And the best way to do that is to retreat, as Timothy said.

But our withdrawal takes a heavy toll on us. The more we close ourselves off, the more we begin thinking that if our friends really knew us, if we spilled all our secrets, they wouldn't want anything to do with us. Living with an alcoholic makes us feel lousy about ourselves. The alcoholic usually is in no condition to meet our needs, and our sober parent, as we'll explore in greater depth later, is often so consumed by her efforts to stop the drinking that she's not there for us either. Our self-esteem plummets as a result, and it only stands to reason that if we don't think much of our true selves, our friends and the rest of the world can't think much of us either. So we hide and cling to a hope that we won't be "discovered." We keep the secrets stuffed inside, feeling guilty about our lies and excuses and about being a bad friend, and try to silence the solitary voice inside that is crying out to smash the secrets to bits—to share with some caring person the painful private world we've retreated into.

Is it any wonder that we wind up feeling different from everyone else? That we get to thinking that nobody really knows us or understands the hurts we feel? "I was always worried about getting too close to my friends," Timothy went on, "because sooner or later the subject of my parents would come up. I wanted to avoid that so I had to keep them at arm's length."

"On the outside, everything looks nice and normal with our family," says Karen. "We live in a nice house and a nice neighborhood. But that's just appearances, because inside what's going on is crazy. Lots of drinking, fighting, craziness. You can't let anybody know what it's really like."

The instinct to keep mum about the drinking problem even extends to our families. Naturally we can't hide it from them as we can from outsiders, but most of us still drape a veil of silence over the subject. "Mostly we all just clammed up and shied away from it," says John of his family's reaction to his mother's drinking problem. "My dad said he'd take care of it and that was it. But it only got worse."

"There were so many secrets you had to keep," echoes Maggie. "My mother's drinking wasn't to be mentioned. My father was so in love with her he refused to see the problem. He exploded like a volcano if you brought it up. Nobody else wanted to talk about it either. I could talk to my sisters a little bit, I guess, but that was it."

What causes most of us to clam up, as John said, is fear. We're terrified of what's going on around us, and somehow we have a sense that if we hide from it and don't talk about it, maybe it'll just go away. More than anything, we want to deny the existence of the drinking problem. And when it gets to the point that it simply can't be denied, we try to escape from it by never opening up to one another about it.

It's important for us to be aware of the harm we do ourselves by suffering in silence. It closes us off, slowly building a wall that sets us apart from the rest of the world. We do it because it feels safe, but the truth is that living behind our self-built wall is especially unsafe, because it makes us feel different and alone and feeds our fear that nobody could ever understand our pain. But that fear, instilled by living with a very frightening disease, is groundless. There are plenty of us out there who understand, who have felt every bit as "different" and isolated. By recognizing that retreating behind this wall is an almost universal reaction to the disease, we can let go of the secrets and share our feelings with others who care for us.

Breaking Down the Wall

Opening up can be difficult in the beginning, I know. When you've bottled feelings up for a long time it can feel as though it's a huge risk to let them out. But take it from a champion bottler and wall-builder, it's a risk well worth taking.

It was to Bill, my doctor friend whom I talked about earlier, that I first opened up. It happened after I'd lived with the problem for a couple of years, at least, and I could sense, even though I was afraid to talk about it, that my withdrawal was getting out of control. I was growing more isolated practically every day. I lived with a knot in my stomach and with what felt like the weight of the world on my shoulders. I needed to share, and I think Bill sensed it. I knew a little of his experiences living with a problem drinker, but we began talking about alcoholism more and more. I learned that he went to a support group called Alateen, a worldwide network of teenagers who live or have lived with an alcoholic. (Probably the single best resource for those of us with an alcoholic parent, Alateen costs nothing to join, and the only qualification you need is to be affected by a problem drinker. Most communities have weekly meetings, often in schools or churches; consult the Appendix for further details.) With Bill's encouragement, I went with him to an Alateen meeting.

The first thing that struck me was how honest people were. You got the feeling nobody had the need to keep secrets. The more I listened, the more I couldn't help but see that these other kids were facing many of the same troubles at home that I was. They, too, had their own horror stories, but one of the things that impressed me most as I continued going was that the meetings weren't just a forum for a bunch of people complaining about what the alcoholic did or didn't do. They weren't about people feeling like victims and sitting around feeling sorry for themselves. They were about strength and hope—about looking into ourselves and searching for attitudes and actions that can make our lives better, regardless of whether the problem drinker is still at it. A great amount of this book has been drawn, directly and indirectly, from the help and hope I've received from going to meetings—first at Alateen and today at Al-Anon, the counterpart program for adults which works in the same way.

I wholeheartedly encourage any young person affected by a drinking problem to go to Alateen. But the larger point here is that, whether it's through Alateen, a private counselor or therapist, a trusted teacher or clergyman or even a close friend, you're going to feel a lot better by knocking down the wall and talking about how you feel about things at home. A deep sense of relief will begin taking hold. "Talking to my friends was a big plus," said Timothy. "They were real understanding. It helped me out a lot. It put things more in focus. And it made us a lot closer because I talked to them about my innermost feelings."

Maggie felt the same way. "When I started being more open I began to realize a lot of people had things in common with me. I let my friends know I had problems and that I was seeing a psychiatrist. And talking to him helped me see how much I was being affected by my mother's drinking problem. I started to feel more secure about myself. Instead of being ashamed of my problems, I tried to think about how talking about it was going to help me feel better. Life began to feel like it was falling together instead of falling apart."

Opening up isn't going to make your problems go away instantly. And it's not going to make the alcoholic sober. But while it isn't magic, it *is* a critical step to finding healthier ways of coping with your parent's drinking problem.

OTHER NEGATIVE EFFECTS

Slowly, subtly, the destructive environment we feel trapped in begins showing itself in many of our thoughts and feelings. So subtle is the process that for most of us it takes a long time to recognize the changes. But they're there—if we look honestly and closely enough—and it's important to see them, because trying to fight the changes or pretending they don't exist will only make matters worse for us.

One surefire sign of our inner turbulence is overreacting to situations. We often become hypersensitive, taking offense at offhand remarks that previously we would've easily brushed aside. We get angry or hurt by even trivial annoyances. One person I talked with described herself as "a raw nerve," never knowing what might hurt her next. It's a good description, I think.

Looking back, I see many instances where I got all worked up over piddling issues. One summer, for example, my friends and I were hard at work building a complicated treehouse in the woods near my house. We went at it long and hard every day. In the midst of our effort, I went off on a long-planned two-week trip, and my friends assured me the work would continue apace. When I got back I found that about two nails had been hammered in my absence. The weather hadn't been so good and things came up, and they just couldn't get much done. Certainly I had every right to feel disappointed. But forget that—I was crushed. I felt abandoned, like they'd all deserted me and didn't care how important the project was to me. A small episode, really, but it reveals how affected I was by the alcoholism at home. I was way oversensitive. My feelings were out of whack. And I don't think we need a psychologist to tell us that because in a very real way I *was* abandoned by my parents, I was extremely sensitive to even the most remote sign that others who were closest to me—my friends—were abandoning me too. Of course, they were doing no such thing. They were terrific friends and always had been. But living with my private fears and hurts left me feeling like a gaping wound, ready to be hurt.

I also took everything personally. People could say something quite harmless, yet I would find a way to take it as an insult. At basketball practice once, I overheard a friend and teammate complimenting another of our teammates. A little while later, I asked my friend, "Why do you think he's a better shooter than me?" He snapped back, "What is it with you? You've got a ridiculous persecution complex lately." It hurt to hear, but he was right. I was embarrassed by my reaction. How could I take it as a slight to me that someone else was praised? It shows how truly needy I was of support and attention—again because I was getting none of those things at home.

"I can explode at the slightest thing," adds Timothy. "I never know what's going to set me off. If any of my friends mentions drinking or parents, it's like a switch goes off and I want to lash out at him. Sometimes I want to jump up and hit him. It's weird. I get overcritical of people a lot of times. I'll say, 'What are you doing? What's wrong with you?' Tension just builds up. The outbursts come from holding all this stuff in. Sometimes I even take it out on the cat and kick it or throw it across the room. And then I feel awful and think, 'What have you done? Look at what you've done.'"

A BLOCK TO PROGRESS

One of the reasons we sometimes have difficulty recognizing how the disease is affecting us is because our focus, as we've seen, is almost always on the alcoholic. When we're not around him, we worry about whether he's drunk, and if he's not, how soon he will be. When we are around him, we worry about how to stop him from getting drunker or from yelling at others in the family. "I'm like Sherlock Holmes," says Bryan. "I'll find those bottles no matter where they're hidden. No alcoholic can fool me." Bryan, like many of us, has spent much of his time playing a futile game of hide-and-seek with the alcoholic, hoping to prevail by finding the secret stashes and outwitting the drinker.

Such an obsession turns our mental and emotional outlook toward the alcoholic and away from ourselves. It slows our personal growth to a crawl—and sometimes stops it altogether. We lose track of our inner selves. Instead of trying to resolve our own problems and taking positive actions to help ourselves, we often get mired in a state where all we're doing is thinking of the alcoholic and of ways to control him. Life revolves around the bottle, and the longer it does, the less attention we pay to our own needs and feelings.

My feelings of being persecuted and overly sensitive were things I realized only well after the fact. Living with the disease had turned virtually all my attention to the drinking. I had little time or energy left for understanding myself better, or for coming up with plans or solutions to lessen my unhappiness. It wasn't until I was able to share my feelings and experiences with others that I came to see that my personal progress would remain at a standstill until I shifted the focus to myself. I realized that only by paying attention to me—to my feelings and thoughts—could I begin to make constructive changes in my life. A common theme I've uncovered in conversations with people affected by alcoholism is how nothing ever changes in their situations. They face the same problems, the same fights, the same lies and cover-ups. I felt that way too. It was a merry-go-round—make it a sad-go-round—and I sure felt as though I wasn't ever getting off.

What we need to understand is that our wheels will continue to spin as long as we remain grimly fixated on the drinker and his drinking. This fixation is a big, nasty part of the family disease of alcoholism. Seeing it at work in our own lives allows room for positive changes and actions. "I'm just beginning to give up worrying about it all the time," says Timothy. "I used to do it 24 hours a day. I would sit in school and worry whether my mom would be drunk when I got home. It was with me constantly. There wasn't room for anything else. It interfered with everything I wanted to do. I had to stop worrying and get on with my own life."

That's the best advice we could ever hope to get. If worrying accomplished anything, if it improved any aspect of our situations, that would be one thing; the fact is that it accomplishes nothing. All it does is increase our burdens and stop us from doing things for ourselves.

I know letting go of worrying is much easier said than done. It feels as though we have no choice, that it's practically an obligation because we love our alcoholic parent and are so concerned for his well-being. But worrying isn't an obligation—we do have choice.

Right now it may seem out of the question that you could ever not be worried or tense about what's going on at home. But it can be done; I know because I've done it. For a long time my entire life was hitched to what kind of shape my mother was in. If she happened to be sober or not too far gone, the day might be acceptable. If she was completely out of it, as was more often the case, forget it. I'd build my walls, retreat to my room, and spend most of the time alone, afraid, and confused.

But I've learned that we don't have to tie up our own lives to the daily state of the alcoholic. Indeed, doing so only invites more harmful feelings, increasing our worry and tension and filling us with a full-time obsession with a disease that we cannot control.

This concept of separating ourselves emotionally from the ups and downs of our parent's drinking is commonly known as detachment. It's a key idea that we'll be returning to again and again, starting with the next chapter. What it means, in essence, is letting go of our natural impulse to worry, to get in there and fight the disease and find one way or another to stop it. It means coming to terms with the things we've looked at in this chapter—how living with a parent's drinking problem has affected us, and finding ways to deal with those affects. It means looking at and caring for ourselves, instead of devoting our life's energy to dreaded thoughts of what will become of the alcoholic, the family—and us. And it means exactly what Timothy expressed so perfectly: getting on with our own lives.

The idea of detaching struck me as selfish and uncaring when I first heard it expressed. "What do you mean, get on with my own life?" I thought. "What about my mother? Am I supposed to just forget her, forget how much I love her?" What I learned is that detaching from the problem doesn't mean you love the alcoholic any less. It doesn't mean you're selfish or disloyal. It's just the best way we know of getting around a highly damaging affect of the disease—namely, the way we become hopelessly entangled with alcohol and with how our parent happens to be that day. It's our way of doing something positive and realistic. By detaching, we're admitting we can't control the problem, that our constant worrying is getting us nowhere and that we're best off turning our focus to things that can make us feel better.

Maybe that means simply making ourselves busier, taking up a hobby or joining a club to help keep our minds off things at home. Maybe it means breaking down our walls and talking with a counselor or going to Alateen meetings. Or it may mean just hanging around listening to records with friends or accepting an invitation to a party or dance—doing something to have fun. The point is, for us to feel better, we're the ones who must look after our own needs. Nobody is going to come along and whisk us out of our dead-end world of worry and confusion.

No, we can't do anything about how much the alcoholic drinks. But yes, we can do things to limit the damage the disease inflicts on us. We have to help ourselves. We have to be our own best friends. We're worth it.

Detaching from the Disease | 4

One thing became clearer and clearer to me as I went on living with an alcoholic: The more I understood the disease, the more I could cope with it and protect myself from many of its most painful consequences. It was almost as though greater understanding provided an umbrella for me—something I could open up and use to shield me from the trouble that was pouring down all around me.

Learning that alcoholism wasn't anything I could cause, control or cure was·one big step in providing shelter for myself. Another was learning to detach from the disease—making a conscious effort to separate myself emotionally from the ugly things that can happen when the problem drinker is active. Let's look at how we can succeed at this detachment process—and make ourselves less vulnerable to getting hurt.

LETTING GO OF LIES AND BROKEN PROMISES

One of the first things we look to our parents for is the truth. If we can't get the straight story from them, who can we get it from? If their word isn't good, whose is?

Chris remembers a time when his father, who recently had moved out of the home, was supposed to spend the day with him and his sister. "We made big plans and we really were looking forward to it," said Chris. "But then my father showed up late and he was so drunk he could barely drive. He wound up pulling off to the side of the road and told us to go off and play. It was a four-lane highway with a huge hill on one side. By this time it was night. We had to cross the road and we found a policeman, who took us to the barracks and arranged for our mother to pick us up." Chris told the story in an even, almost matter-of-fact voice, but beneath the smooth exterior there seemed to be an inner voice, a look in the eyes that was crying out, "How could you have done this to us? How could you care so little?"

John also felt hurt about not being able to trust his alcoholic parent. "My mom was always making promises to stop," he said. "She'd talk about how everything was going to be fine, and that soon it would be just like the old days when she was sober. But she could never do it and keep her promises. Sometimes for a day or two she'd stop, but you could see she was very uncomfortable and really wanted to drink. You could never trust her. She lied all the time and hid drinks and bottles all over."

Most of us have shared similar hurts and letdowns. We learn the hard way that when a drinking problem enters the picture, telling the truth goes out. That certainly was the case in my situation. Life began to seem like one huge deception. There were lies about what my mother was drinking (one of her favorite ploys was to put liquor in a cup and pass it off as coffee), how much she'd had, when she'd started, and broken promises galore about how tomorrow or the day after would be much better. Indeed, the longer we live with an alcoholic parent, the more painfully apparent it becomes that promises aren't worth an empty glass and that the alcoholic will make any excuse, invent any story, that might get us off his back and ensure that he can keep the flow of alcohol going. The problem drinker makes vows to stop or cut back, and cannot; he arranges a trip or special outing, and can't go because he's drunk; he promises to help with your homework or attend the opening night of the class play, but it never happens. He says things will soon be better, that he's just going through a tough time, but things only get worse and life at home only gets grimmer. The unfortunate fact is that lies and unkept promises are commonplace in alcoholic homes.

So what can we do? We can remind ourselves continuously that our parent isn't doing this willfully or maliciously just to hurt us. I know how hard this can be to accept because lots of times the lie or broken promise *does* seem willful. There were times when I was convinced my mother was going out of her way to hurt me, like the time she got drunk knowing full well I was bringing my girlfriend over for the first time. "Don't worry," she said beforehand. "I'll be fine." Foolishly, I believed her. I wanted to believe her. What I wasn't taking into account was that the disease was beyond her control, and all the solemn vows in the world weren't going to change that. By losing sight of this fact and taking her at her word, I left myself open for pain. I took it personally. She lied to me, broke her promise. Disappointment and anger welled up inside me, provoking that common, pained refrain: "How could you do this *to me*?"

But the problem drinker isn't doing it *to us*. He almost certainly has no desire to hurt us, and quite likely has intentions as pure as new snow. But good intentions are no match for alcoholism. The disease overpowers them because the compulsion to drink is the most important thing in the alcoholic's life. It completely skews your parent's judgment and good sense. It makes a person who's 100-percent dependable, as my mother is, into someone who can't be counted on to come through in even the smallest of ways. Everything takes a back seat to the craving to drink, and we can't forget that if we want to avoid living with constant hurt and anger. Your parent is not breaking promises or lying to you on purpose. Nor is he doing it simply because he'd rather drink than be a good, reliable parent. He's doing it because he *has* to drink. That is his disease, and the better we're able to keep that in mind, the less we'll be battered by painful feelings. Hard as it sometimes was, I kept telling myself, "I can't count on my mother as long as her disease is active. I can't trust her word, and I can't depend on her to be there for me. This isn't because she's a liar, or a terrible person. It's because she is an alcoholic."

LETTING GO OF SHAME AND EMBARRASSMENT

"I moved to a new school in seventh grade," recalls Elise. "My mother wanted me to have a birthday party and invite my new friends. I didn't want to have a party that much but she insisted. Everyone came over and I had a terrible time. My mother was drunk. It was really obvious. I just wanted to go someplace and hide."

John felt much the same way the time his friends from the neighborhood came over for a barbecue and his mother fell on her face while carrying a plate of food. "I got really mad and left the house," said John. "It was the worst for me when people were over. My mother would be in the kitchen doing the cooking and she'd always have a bottle in there with her. It was horrible just to watch her get worse. She'd start slurring her words and stumbling and it was awful. I never had kids over after that because I was afraid she'd get drunk and I felt ashamed."

"There was one time I remember wanting to die," recalls Timothy. "My mother was driving my friends and me home from the movies. She was drunk and I knew it, but I was just hoping that they wouldn't notice. But she was all over the road. It was terrifying. I felt helpless. I didn't know what to do. Finally, one of my friends told her to pull the car over and she did, and they all piled out. God, I just wished I was a million miles away."

Feelings of shame and embarrassment are not

uncommon when you live with an alcoholic parent. They are a natural response to the hurt that's caused when the problem is played out before other people. For me, the public airing of the drinking problem was the most dreaded fear of all. It was a humiliating announcement to the world that I had a drunk for a mother. I tried everything I could think of to keep the problem private. Like John, I was always taking measures to steer my friends away from coming over. I'd make up stories about someone in the family being sick or tired or in a bad mood. I didn't even care that much if they believed me; all I cared about was that they not see my mother stumbling around the house drunk.

Of course, my efforts to keep the drinking problem a family secret were doomed to failure. Alcoholism tends to be a disease that can't stay unnoticed for long. My mother would go to a neighbor's house and ask for liquor. My parents would go to parties and my mother would drink to the point of incoherence or unconsciousness. But probably my most vivid memory of the "secret" getting out was on parents' night at my high school, where teachers meet with moms and dads to talk about the classwork and how kids are progressing. My mother started drinking in the late afternoon. I knew she'd be loaded by the time she was due at school. I desperately tried to talk her out of going, but she would hear nothing of it. She saw it as her duty; she was trying to be a good parent. Off she went—certainly in no condition to drive—and I stayed home in my room, fearful of what my teachers would think of me after seeing her in such a state.

No insight or piece of advice can turn a humiliating experience into a pleasant one. You want to feel proud of your parents and be able to look up to them. It hurts when your parent's behavior is such that you can't do that, when you feel that you have to hide your parent from other people in your world. It hurts even more when your alcoholic parent does something that makes you want to crawl under the nearest rock.

But you *can* pull yourself back from those humiliating moments. Here, too, the key is separating your parent, the person you love, from the horrible disease that has overtaken his life, ruined his judgment and that is causing him to do things that hurt you. Once you can draw this distinction, you can begin to see that there isn't anything for you personally to feel ashamed of. Your parent has a disease—he cannot control his drinking. His behavior under the influence may make you uncomfortable, but the fact that he has a disease is no reason to feel shame. Remember we're not talking about a moral issue here. Your parent isn't a lush or a horrible person; it's not that he *won't* control his drinking, it's that he *can't*. It's not your fault, it's not your parent's, it's not anybody's.

When you get right down to it, *we* leave ourselves open to feeling shame and embarrassment by failing truly to believe that the problem is a disease and attributing it instead to a lack of willpower. Ask yourself, do you think deep down that if your parent really wanted to, he could stop drinking? That the only thing that's stopping him is that he doesn't want to badly enough, and that it's his fault as a result? If the answers are yes, then you haven't yet been able to accept the disease concept. And it can be a very hard thing to accept. It took me a long time to get past thinking that my mother was nothing other than a "bad girl" whenever she got drunk, particularly when she acted up in front of other people. What does that attitude say about my deepest feelings about her drinking? That I still wasn't accepting the fact that she had no control over it. Thinking of her in those terms, I was saying in effect that she was simply misbehaving, much as someone should know better than to make a tasteless remark or act in a childish manner.

I went to work on my attitude. With the help of my friend Bill and friends I met in Alateen, I kept hammering into my head that there was no cause to feel ashamed or embarrassed by my mother's drinking. I tried hard to restrain the emotions emerging from the daily mishaps and chaos I was living with. This isn't to say that I was any happier about it when an awkward incident occurred—just that I kept on working to accept fully that the scene was not the result of my mother's poor judgment, but of an illness that she was powerless to control. I tried hard to depersonalize the situation, and even though it didn't work magic, it did work. It made me feel better. I began to detach from those horrible, awkward moments, and I began to stop seeing the scenes as more evidence of my mother not caring about my feelings.

I knew I'd made progress in my own thinking when I brought a friend home from college one weekend. We entered the house and I called for my mother. No answer. The car was in the garage so I knew she was home. I sensed things were not going to be okay, and I was right. We walked upstairs and there she was, sprawled unconscious at the top of the stairs. Shame and embarrassment almost automatically started welling up before I talked to myself about detachment. "I have no reason to be ashamed," I kept telling myself. "My mother is a sick person. She has no control over her drinking. It is no reflection on me. I wish things were different and that she had welcomed us in a different way, but I can't do anything to change it. I have to let go of it."

Gradually my feelings eased. The knot in my stomach slowly unwound. I realized I didn't have to be a prisoner of the first rush of feelings that I'd always been flooded with. I realized I didn't have to let her drunken state cast a pall over my life. I could still enjoy spending time with my friend, I told myself. And I was right.

It's probably no accident that this healing process occurred when it did, with this particular friend near at hand, because he was someone I'd shared a lot of my feelings with. His mom also is an alcoholic and we'd talked about the disease at great length. He understood that I had no control over what condition my mom would be in. Having met my mother previously when she'd been sober, he also knew how kind and hospitable she could be, so that he was prepared not to take the lack of welcome personally. Finally, he knew, as I did, that when you live with an alcoholic, unpredictability is the norm, and that awkward moments and potentially painful situations are always right around the corner.

This is something to feel sad about; it is a sad and sometimes tragic disease. But it is not something to feel ashamed of. A few years earlier, probably six months earlier, I would've been a wreck if confronted with such a scene. I probably would have told my friend to leave and would've let my own life and feelings get twisted and dragged down to despair. I felt good that I didn't allow that to happen. I felt good that I was able to detach from the sickness and make a choice to carry my life forward. It took a lot of mental legwork. But no effort could've been for a worthier cause.

PARENT AS CHILD

One of the effects of alcoholism is to stunt a person's emotional growth. Talking to problem drinkers, one often hears them speak about regressing to child-like ways or refer to themselves as kids who never grew up.

This puts us in a difficult and often painful spot. Our parents are our primary role models, and when drinking interferes with the way they meet that role, it's deeply unsettling at the very least. It can make us confused or angry or both. With much sadness and an undercurrent of disgust, Diane told of how her father behaved after a particularly bad night. "He'd come home with presents for me," she said. "If I wasn't home he'd put them on my bed. He obviously felt very guilty. It was a bribe, like he was buying things just to win me over and I didn't like it. I didn't want his presents. I never opened them. I just wanted a normal father."

Sometimes, too, your parent might want the attention usually demanded by a child. "My dad gets really lonely when he drinks," says Kent. "He never wants to be left alone, so when I go out to see my friends he gets angry and threatens me. Sometimes he says he'll never let me back in the house again if I go out." I heard that a lot as well. My mom became starved for affection and attention when she was drinking. She was like an infant. There were times I felt as though I couldn't even leave the room without her howling for me to come back. And no matter what I said or did, it never seemed to be enough for her. She always needed more.

It hurt a lot to see her that way, not only because she was pathetic, but also because she would stop at nothing to get her way. If she thought belligerence would work, she was belligerent. If she thought sentimentality would work, she was sentimental. She was overwhelmed by her neediness, whether for attention, emotional support, a new supply of liquor or whatever. She'd even resort to blackmail to meet her needs. "If you don't stay and keep me company I'm going to drink a lot more," she'd sometimes say. Other times it would be: "If you don't go to the liquor store I'll go myself." What could I do? Her getting behind the wheel was a ticket to disaster.

It made me angry to feel so manipulated. I also felt angry that she was so needy and child-like. It can really twist you up inside to see your parent acting like a four-year-old. Some of the most powerful responses from the young people I've talked with were stirred by feelings of having "to be a parent to their parent." That's not the way it's supposed to be. "I feel like I never had a childhood," said Karen, a child of two alcoholics, echoing words I heard from many others. "I had to be the responsible one or nothing ever would've gotten done. My little sister is only two years younger than me, but I was like her mother. I felt protective and that I had to take care of her. But nobody took care of me."

Most of us share Karen's feelings of being neglected. The compulsion to drink is pretty much a full-time endeavor. It doesn't leave much room for giving us attention or finding out about our needs. We wind up feeling cheated, and as though we're not a very high priority in our parent's life. "I used to go to Boy Scouts," said Roger, "and I remember being jealous because all the other guys had their fathers with them. Mine dropped me off at the door and took off for the bar."

It's extremely hard not to take your parent's neglect to heart and equally difficult not holding it against him for abandoning his parental role and acting like a little kid. But these are things we must try to do for *our own sake*. Nothing less than our peace of mind is at stake. And again, just as with the hurts brought on by not being able to trust your parent or feeling ashamed of his behavior, the key is drawing a line between your parent, the person, and the disease he is ravaged by. As we've discussed before, the behavior that inflicts pain on you and troubles your life is not adopted willfully. Your parent does not seek intentionally to screw up your life by neglecting you or by acting like a kid. Alcoholism has reduced his existence to that sorry state. It's okay to feel cheated because you are being cheated. More than anything, I wanted my mother to be as she once was, like most of my friends' mothers. But we can't allow our bruised feelings to turn into blame, or to fall into thinking that our parent's failings amount to a lack of love. The more you're able to keep this in mind and the better you become at not taking personally the whole wicked web of the disease's ill effects—the lies, the broken promises, the public scenes, the neglect—the saner and healthier your life will be.

Your Sober
Parent|5

When a drinking problem leaves one of our parents unable to supply the support and guidance we need, it's only natural to look to the other parent (our sober parent, except for those with two alcoholic parents) to fill the void. Often this isn't even a conscious decision; it's simply a product of our increasing awareness that the problem drinker's life has become so tightly wrapped around the bottle that there's room for little else, us included. So we look for someone who does have room for us.

Think for a moment of your parents as two separate wells. You're used to drawing strength and direction from each, but once an alcohol problem appears, you quickly learn that there's little or nothing to be drawn from that well any longer. So instinctively you turn to the other. The trouble is that even though the second well does have a supply of some of the things you're looking for, in many instances it can't provide everything you need. Forced to fulfill the function of both wells, it is often strained by the heavy demand, and sometimes even runs dry for short periods. Either way, it is unable to function as effectively as it could when it was working in tandem with the other.

UNDERSTANDING YOUR SOBER PARENT'S POSITION

In examining alcoholism as a family disease, we've already looked at how the illness works its way into each family member, fostering unhealthy attitudes and behavior. But while the negative impact touches all of us, it's important to see that the sober parent has a special burden, because almost inevitably she feels she must be two parents in one. Sensing the harm and trauma that is being inflicted on us, she seeks to shield us from it as best she can. This is an enormous pressure, but by no means the only one she faces. She also may be forced to manage the family finances (often an onerous task, since a serious drinking problem is frequently accompanied by serious money troubles when the alcoholic loses his job, squanders money, incurs big medical bills, etc.), handle all domestic duties singlehandedly and try her best to accomplish something that's all but impossible—to keep the whole family functioning and moving along in spite of the awful disease in its midst. On top of all this, your other parent almost unquestionably faces the added pressure of a burgeoning marital problem. Even if your parents don't argue in front of you, a drinking problem usually causes tensions between a husband and wife. Serious differences may occur over the alcoholic's neglect of the kids, the family's worsening financial picture and the amount of work days the drinker has been missing. But the biggest battle of all, of course, is over the bottle itself; typically, the strains stem from the sober parent accusing, nagging, scolding or getting angry at the drinker, and the drinker getting angry back, accusing her of over-reacting and denying the existence of any alcohol problem.

Denial at Work

In almost every home, the initial response to the mounting pressures brought on by a drinking problem is to hide: ignore the overwhelming evidence, gloss over the fear and find some other trouble area—anything but alcohol—as the source of friction. We've already talked about the power of denial and how everyone in the family—not just the problem drinker—seeks to avoid the truth. Deep down, your sober parent knows better, just as the alcoholic knows better. But the reality of the situation is too painful and too frightening to face, so she, too, finds ways to delude herself about the true nature and scope of the trouble. The same qualities that make the problem terrifying to us make it the same way for our sober parent. She's afraid because she doesn't know how to deal with it. She's afraid because no matter what she does, she can't control it. She's afraid because she never knows what to expect, whether the alcoholic will come home drunk or have an accident or want to pick a fight. She's afraid because she thinks of it as a huge disgrace and worries about neighbors and friends finding out about it. So instead of acknowledging the drinking problem, the family troubles are attributed to something else. Maybe you've heard some of the following:

"Daddy's going through a difficult time at work."

"Mom just hasn't been herself ever since Grandpa passed away."

"Your father and I have been having some disagreements, but we're going to straighten things out soon."

"Mom's under a lot of pressure these days. Just try to be extra nice to her and help her as much as you can, and everything'll be fine."

From our vantage point, it's very difficult to take when our non-drinking parent seems to be pretending the problem doesn't exist. It's hard enough that we can't trust our drinking parent, but it's that much worse when we know we're not getting the truth from the other one. We want to believe our sober parent when she makes excuses and acts as if there's no drinking problem, but inside we know that there most definitely is a problem, and the charade just adds to our confusion. Maggie describes her situation this way:

> I never wanted to admit my mother's drinking, but eventually there wasn't any way around it. Every single night she would fall asleep in front of the TV, and the whole thing was very scary. I felt alone and wanted to talk about it with my father, but he made it clear this was not to be discussed. He'd come home, and forget it! It would be 9 o'clock and he'd say to my mother, "Would you like a drink, honey?" It was so frustrating. He would never admit the real problem was her drinking. When she was sick in bed and hung over he would baby her and say, "Oh, your mother's sick, go get her a cup of coffee or whatever." He just seemed to ignore it. It made me angry. I think his attitude only made things worse.

The denial wasn't as fierce in my own situation, mostly because the problem was so obvious that it simply couldn't be overlooked. So instead of denying it outright, my sober parent—my father—sought to minimize it. One night during a period when the drinking was especially bad, I remember going to him, looking for answers and comfort. "How long can this go on? What can we do?" I asked. He said, "Things are going to get better real soon. We're going to have this problem taken care of by the end of February."

Much as I wanted to believe him, I knew he wasn't telling the truth. The end of February was six weeks away. He probably wanted to believe his words more than anything, and I'm sure he meant well. But it hurt to have the problem treated so casually, as though a spell of magic would come along and make it disappear. My worries mounted, my burden grew heavier, because I realized that even my sober parent didn't have a clue as to how to deal with the problem.

YOUR PARENT'S OBSESSION

"I felt like neither of my parents were there when my father was drinking," says Diane. "My mother barely had any time for me. Either she was fighting with my father or hiding or looking for his bottles, and that was about all that went on. I was her assistant; I would help her find bottles. But there wasn't anything else we really did together."

Understanding your sober parent's plight is important for coping with your own feelings. The reason is that sometimes the lack of attention from the non-drinker hurts us more than the behavior of the alcoholic. It quickly becomes obvious to us that we can't expect much from the alcoholic. We can see all too clearly when he's drunk and that alcohol is controlling his life. But the effects of the family disease on our sober parent aren't nearly as visible. And since we know our other parent isn't drunk, we automatically expect more from her. Hurt results when those expectations are not met.

We have to remember that our sober parent is as obsessed with the drinking as the alcoholic. As determined as the drinker is to keep at it, the non-drinker is equally determined to stop it. And as Diane observed, that endeavor leaves little room for anything else. Until your sober parent comes to realize the futility of her efforts, that she cannot control the alcoholic's drive to drink, her life will revolve almost exclusively around her schemes to outwit the alcoholic and keep him from getting drunk. Her misdirected energy will allow little time for you.

Here, as in our dealings with the alcoholic, we have to condition ourselves not to take it personally. Your sober parent undoubtedly has noble intentions; she's doing what she thinks is best for you and the whole family by trying so hard to stop the drinking. She isn't slighting you on purpose; it's simply a case of allowing herself to be consumed by a quest to control or cure the problem.

Sometimes the non-drinking parent will leave home altogether, either temporarily or permanently. This happens more frequently when the alcoholic is your mother (studies have shown that women are much more likely to stay with an alcoholic spouse than men are), my experience being a case in point. My father came and went a number of times, but eventually decided he could no longer live with my mother while she was drinking. So he left for good.

For those of us who have had a parent leave, it's vital to see the departure in the context of the alcohol problem. Again, this is not something to be taken as a personal slap in the face. Your parent's leaving is not because he or she doesn't care about you; it's because the frustration, helplessness and stress from living with the alcoholic has simply gotten to be too much. Sometimes a separation can actually be the best thing for you and your parents; it was in our situation. My mother had a great amount of pent-up anger toward my father, and it came out in torrents when she was drunk and he was anywhere nearby. The fighting, crying, screaming, it all reached a point that I could barely stand anymore. I found myself hoping he would come home late or not at all. So when my father decided to leave, I was actually relieved in a way. The problem was still there, but at least things were a little quieter.

But whether the circumstances at home are better or worse if the sober parent leaves, we need to keep in mind that the non-drinkers are victims of the disease, just as we are. It stirs powerful and negative reactions in them exactly as it does in us. Their thinking becomes twisted and their minds become preoccupied. All of these changes have nothing to do with their feelings for us. They are typical responses from a person who shares our confusion and helplessness and who feels the added pressure—since she's your parent—to take care of the problem not only for her own sake, but for yours as well.

CHANGES IN YOUR SOBER PARENT

The stress your non-drinking parent is experiencing may well be causing significant changes in her personality and in the way she treats you. Perhaps you're noticing that she's more short-tempered with you than she was before. Maybe she's getting on your case over things you do or don't do—leaving dishes in the sink, asking for a ride on her busiest day, doing your homework in front of the TV—that previously would've been overlooked. Probably you're getting a lot of conflicting signals. One day your parent may be all sweetness and the next be jumping on you for not refilling the ice cube tray.

You also may feel your sober parent is much harder and more demanding on you than before the drinking got bad. What often happens is that your non-drinking parent will take out on you the frustration and helplessness she feels over the drinking. She desperately wants something to feel good about, so she may unconsciously be demanding that you be a better kid—do better in school, be more obedient and responsible, be the star athlete or piano player, etc. Your performance gives her something to latch onto, a way to deflect the pain of living with a drunken spouse. "My parents never gave me much credit for anything I did," recalls Roy. "I didn't expect it from my father because he was drunk so much, but my mother didn't give me any either. I felt like I never measured up to what she expected from me. She always bugged me about my grades, which weren't bad at all, so I tried real hard and brought home something like four A's and a B. And she said, "Why did you get a B?"

Sometimes the pressures may affect your sober parent in a different way, and she'll adopt a martyr's attitude. She might say things like, "Nobody appreciates the things that I do;" "I'm tired of being everybody's slave;" "Nobody cares about my problems;" "I'm going through all this hell for you, I want you to know that." She may try to make you feel guilty for not being nicer to her, or for not being understanding enough. Then if she succeeds and makes you feel bad, perhaps even making you cry, she may turn around and apologize, feeling guilty herself for coming down so hard on you.

It's hard dealing with such inconsistency, but it's behavior we have to expect and try to accept. While we don't have to like the way we're being treated, we can do our best to understand that our sober parent feels under siege and is trying hard to hold everything together. Such understanding will help us not take to heart the mood swings and unpredictability. It also may help to know that your sober parent probably has no more of an idea how she'll respond to a given situation than you do. Her impatience or bad mood isn't premeditated; it's a spur-of-the-moment reaction that has a lot more to do with the pressure she's feeling than whatever it is you're doing. Bear in mind that just like us, she feels emotionally battered by the topsy-turvy experience of living with the alcoholic. If things were more tranquil last night, if the alcoholic has gone on the wagon for a few days, your sober parent may be more tolerant, patient and relaxed. On the other hand, if you heard your parents shouting at each other at two in the morning or if the situation seems to be getting worse, then she's probably going to be near the end of her rope.

What we need to remember, no matter how things are on a particular day, is that everyone in the family is being subjected to the same strains and stresses. If your sober parent seems different, it's because she is; she is suffering, as we all are, from the family disease of alcoholism.

REALIZING THAT YOU CAN'T RESCUE YOUR SOBER PARENT

A natural response to our sober parent's difficulties is to do our utmost to make things better for her. Doing more household chores, working harder in school, looking after little brothers and sisters—we might do these and other things in the hope of lightening our parent's load and making her feel better. These are constructive actions that can provide relief, and your sober parent will probably appreciate your efforts very much. But we have to be careful about devoting ourselves too much to "fixing" things, about trying too hard to make our sober parent happier.

The reason is that no matter what lengths we go to to make everything better, we cannot do anything about the root of all the distress, the alcoholism. We have to accept that, ultimately, it is not in our power to erase the problem that's weighing so heavily on our sober parent. Why is this so important to keep in mind? Because if we don't, our failure to make a significant improvement can make us feel at fault, as though we're just not much good at anything. Diane, for example, describes how she tried to help her mother. "I wanted so badly to make her feel better," she remembers. "One time when he was drunk my father knocked into a stand and broke a ceramic bowl that was very special to my mom. She started screaming at him and they had a big fight. I picked up all the pieces—there were hundreds of them—and went into my room and spent about four hours gluing it back together. But then when I showed it to her she barely had a reaction."

Her symbolic attempt to put a shattered life back together for her mother went almost completely unnoticed. More than anything, Diane wanted to fix everything for her mother, and when she couldn't do it, she felt crummy about herself, like she couldn't do anything. It was only in talking in depth about the incident and realizing what she was up against that Diane came to see that she was setting herself up for the bad feelings by trying to fix something that wasn't in her power to fix.

A FEW THOUGHTS ABOUT YOUR SIBLINGS

Just as we can easily become hurt or angry by what our sober parent is—or isn't—doing for us, it's also common to feel that way toward our brothers and sisters. If you have an older sibling, for instance, you may be upset that he or she isn't doing anything about the problem, refuses to talk about it or isn't shielding you from the effects of the drinking. Or you may resent the way, as the drinking gets increasingly worse, that your older sibling is acting more and more like a parent—telling you what you can and can't do, punishing you, deciding when you come and go. With the focus of both parents squarely on the bottle, the result often is a serious lapse in family order; rules aren't set, decisions aren't made and the family functions poorly. Often one of the children (typically one of the oldest) will try to fill the void by adopting a parental role and assuming responsiblity for getting things done and restoring some sense of sanity to the home.

You may not like for your brother or sister to behave this way. You may feel angry at him or her for acting high and mighty and for being bossy. Or, if you are the super-responsible one, you may be angry at how the others aren't helping or aren't trying nearly as hard as you are to keep things from falling apart completely.

A number of books detail the various roles that we children of alcoholics unconsciously fall into as a result of the drinking problem. Some of us become almost compulsively responsible; others go the other way and "act out" their unhappiness—whether by letting their studies slide, getting in trouble with the authorities or abusing alcohol or drugs themselves. Still other children of alcoholics may withdraw almost completely, seeming afraid and disinterested in life and rarely venturing out of their private worlds. These specific roles and family interactions don't have a direct bearing on our discussion here, so we're not going into them in great detail. The central point to remember is that each of us—every person who lives or has lived with an alcoholic parent—is profoundly affected by it. The fear, the unpredictability, the shame, the frustration and guilt about not being able to do anything about the problem—the whole dark web of forces that alcoholism evokes—is doing the same thing to your brothers and sisters.

It's important to keep in mind—particularly if you're having problems getting along with your siblings—that a big part of the disease's destructiveness is the way it can rip apart families. Yes, it's a family disease, but it affects different members of the family in different ways. Instead of pulling us together during such a time of stress, the disease often tugs us apart. And the strains in relationships only get compounded by the silence and the denial of the problem. If you try to talk about your feelings, you may find that your sibling cuts you off, changes the subject or disputes what you are saying. You may be working through the denial, coming to terms with your parent's disease, and a brother or sister, still terrified of the drinking problem, may ignore you or become angry with you for being so honest about the situation. He or she simply may not want to hear it, just as you may not want to hear it if *you* are the one denying the problem and a sibling is confronting you with the ugly reality of the problem.

Living with an alcoholic parent can be a relentlessly draining and debilitating experience. Try to keep in mind that the same damage is being done to your brothers and sisters, and that if you're not getting along or if you don't like the way they're reacting to the situation, the hurt and distance you may feel toward them is a function of how the disease affects different people. Remember that you're all in the same boat. Your brothers and sisters can be a huge help to you because, after all, no matter how close you are to someone outside the family, nobody can really know what you're going through as well as someone who is going through it too. If you try to understand that the disease is inflicting damage on your siblings just as it is on you, and try to understand what's behind the attitudes or behavior you don't much care for, you may well find it easier to reach out to them and begin talking openly about your fears and worries. You may discover that your relationships can mend quite rapidly. And you also may discover what comfort and strength can be found in letting go of the silence and isolation and sharing the hurts that all of you are being subjected to.

A FINAL WORD

One parent's drinking problem can cause difficulties in our relationship with the other parent. Without realizing it, we often begin to expect more from our sober parent, looking to her for the attention, affection and support that are almost always lacking in alcoholic homes. But our non-drinking parent feels a tremendous burden. Usually she feels responsible for keeping things functioning and for protecting us from the ugly consequences of the drinking. She often becomes so preoccupied with stopping the drinking that she is unable to meet our needs and expectations. We probably see the pressures affecting her in different ways. She may be moody or short-tempered. She may seem to make unreasonable demands on us. Sometimes, overwhelmed by her inability to improve the situation, she may just break down and cry for no specific reason.

We need to detach from our sober parent, much the way we detach from the alcoholic. We need to take a step back from her words and actions and understand that she's under a great strain and that she probably doesn't intend to be mean or jumpy. Managing to do this is a huge help in depersonalizing the situation at home, in easing the hurts and slights we feel from mistreatment or neglect. Everyone who lives with an alcoholic is affected by the problem, and your non-drinking parent is no exception. She may seem depressed or not herself, even if your relationship with her is fine.

If this is the case, it's great to be supportive and to try to help her in any way you can. But at the same time, remember that it's not your job to wave a magic wand and make things better for her. The root of her unhappiness has nothing to with you or anything you have or haven't done. It has to do with the disease that everyone in the family, in his or her own way, is trying to cope with.

Good Intentions, Bad Results|6

In previous chapters we've looked at how we make futile attempts to stop the alcoholic from drinking. We've talked about our blatant efforts—hiding bottles and pouring them out—as well as more subtle, psychological ploys, such as guilt-peddling, preaching, scolding and otherwise punishing the problem drinker for his naughty ways. We've also discussed that these attempts not only are destined to fail, but also that they actually cause us harm by making us feel like incompetent, ineffective people who can't make even the smallest improvement in the drinking problem.

Of course, we now know that our failure has nothing to do with being incompetent or ineffective. We're contending with a disease that we're utterly powerless over, and the more readily we accept this, the more we'll spare ourselves needless emotional anguish.

There's another big incentive to let go of the urge to control the drinking. And that is that a controlling manner, whether by trying to cut off the liquor supply or by using psychological artillery to punish the drinker, doesn't harm only us; it also does great harm to the alcoholic. In this chapter we're going to see how. And in looking at how *not* to treat the alcoholic, we'll begin discovering constructive ways of how *to* treat him.

HIDING BOTTLES

Probably the most common initial response to a drinking problem is attempting to cut off the alcohol supply. I participated in numerous schemes to that end; perhaps you have too. What good can come of such efforts? None. Indeed, one group of alcoholism scholars have said, "No one act is a bigger waste of time and money."

Our misguided effort only makes the alcoholic that much less inclined to recognize his problem and seek help. It builds enormous resentment within him. "Who are they to hide my bottles?" he thinks angrily. "Why do they hover over me like I'm a little child?" Remember that the problem drinker has surrounded himself with a great wall of denial. Part of the disease is finding any way he can not to admit that he has it. Implicit in his resentful attitude is a feeling that "everything would be fine if they would just leave me alone." Thus he may go on loud and long about how the excessive drinking is our fault, that we're making him feel like a prisoner in his own home. Of course it's not our fault, but he'll do whatever it takes to remove the responsibility from himself, and our ill-fated attempts to control only help him.

Hiding the alcohol also often provokes anger. So rather than perhaps getting closer to a realization of the problems alcohol is creating in his life, his focus is turned to full-blown rage over our intrusion. He dwells on what *we* are doing to him, rather than what *alcohol* is doing to him. His denial pushes him to think of himself as a victim, a poor, misunderstood soul who only wants to relax with a drink—and is getting nothing but harassment from his loved ones. Compounding everything is the fact that usually the alcoholic eagerly accepts our challenge to play the hide-and-seek game with his liquor. He is bent on revenge. "I'll show them" or "They can't outwit me" become his standard ways of thinking of the situation. So again, instead of focusing on what the stuff is doing to him, he's feeling huge amounts of self-pity and devoting himself to a sick competition that produces only losers.

Our goal in relating to the alcoholic is to behave in a way that can help him face the reality of his drinking problem. Controlling him dramatically reduces the chances of that happening. In effect we're treating him like a little kid with our bottle-hiding ploys; our attitude is like that of a parent who catches a four-year-old with a fistful of brownies 10 minutes before dinner. But we need to see that as long as we treat him like a child, someone who can't be trusted and must be hovered over all the time, the more he's going to act like one. It makes him angry and brimming with resentment and, on a deeper level, only makes him feel worse about himself because our actions reaffirm what he knows deep down but cannot yet face: that he can't manage his own life. We do want him to realize that truth, but it's a painful conclusion that must be arrived at by himself. Pushing him toward it doesn't help.

PUNISHING OUTBURSTS

We all know how easy it is to allow ourselves to be hurt by the alcoholic's behavior. A broken promise, a nasty comment, an insensitive remark—these are just a few of the ways the problem drinker can hurt our feelings. When enough of these things have been done over time, what usually happens is that our resentments mount, we snap and then seek revenge, getting even by hurting the alcoholic right back.

One way many of us do this is by not accepting the alcoholic's efforts to patch things up. Diane's father, you'll recall, often would come home after a bad night with an armful of presents. Other times, she said, he would take her for ice cream or buy her candy. Her father desperately wanted to atone for the guilt he felt for being a crummy, drunken father. Diane got back at him by not accepting the gestures. Presents would remain unopened. She would decline offers for the special treats. She wanted to send him an unmistakable message: "No, I don't forgive you."

An even more common method of getting even is scorn, which was a personal favorite of mine. Filled with hurt, I'd strike back with remarks such as, "Did you really have to go and get so drunk last night?" or, "One of these days maybe you'll actually keep one of your promises not to drink." Or more simply, "If you don't care about yourself, don't you at least care about what you're doing to me?"

In all of these statements, I'm throwing the drinking back in the face of the alcoholic. I'm trying to use guilt, ridicule, sarcasm—anything I can come up with to get back at my mother, and to show her my hurt so that she would be moved to clean up her act. Francis was doing the same thing when he held up a bottle and confronted his drunken parent. "You care more about this damn bottle than you do about any of us, don't you? Don't you?!" he shouted. "This is the most important thing in your life—admit it!"

Other times we might plead, cry, scream or simply confront the alcoholic with all the anger we can muster. Remember how Maggie talked of how her constant refrain to her mother was "I hate you." "Why did you even bother going?" bellowed Brian, who was distraught when his mother suffered a relapse after a month-long stay at an alcohol rehabilitation center. "Were you just pretending to learn things there? Was that all you were doing, just going through the motions? I guess so, because you're as much of a drunk now as you were before!"

For a long time, I had an awfully hard time with broken promises; that's what set me off more than anything. Invariably my revenge would be to make a public scene of my hurt. I wanted my mother to know exactly how much I was suffering. Many times I remember getting her to promise she would be on her best behavior. Almost as many times I remember her getting drunk anyway. "How could you do this to me?" I'd cry out. "Why do you humiliate me in front of my friends?"

DETACHMENT TO THE RESCUE

These incidents are all examples of punishing our alcoholic parent. Certainly, living with a problem drinker provokes feelings of wanting to avenge our wounds. But there's more to our reaction than that. On a deeper level what we're really hoping for is to inflict so much hurt on our drinking parent that he will see the trouble he's creating and be motivated to stop it. Even though it isn't conscious, we're clinging to a notion that with an acute and poignant show of pain, it will register with the alcoholic, make him feel terrible and pave the way for brighter days.

Unfortunately, the disease doesn't work that way. If it did, my mother would've been sober about seven years earlier; that's how much energy and emotion I wasted trying to show her once and for all the damage she was doing to herself and the family. I was sure I could make her see the light. I was sure I could lead her out of the mess she was in. I was wrong.

Simply by trying to make my mother feel so bad she would stop, it's clear that I had not truly embraced the disease concept. Indeed, my actions were ignoring that reality altogether. They were saying, "If only I can force her to see how bad things are, she'll want to get better." But forced solutions don't work with alcoholism. We cannot make an alcoholic want to stop drinking. Neither guilt, nor anger, nor scorn can rid a person of this disease, because the drinking has nothing to do with a deliberate effort to hurt us. For our own sanity, we must dispense with any notion that somehow, some way, we can find such a perfect and painful punishment for the alcoholic that something will click inside and move him to stop drinking. Not only is this an utterly false hope, it also leaves us open for even more hurt. For how can we feel anything but worse when we lash out with a torrent of blame and pain, only to have the disease rage on as if we'd never opened our mouths? Our pain, after all, is being ignored. And we turn within and think, "He doesn't care about me even the slightest bit. He's seen how broken up I am about the drinking and still he refuses to do anything." And thus we feel that much more rejected and abandoned.

This is exactly what happened in my situation—before I started working on detachment. There were a few times that I became so overwrought with hurt that I lost myself totally, screaming, crying, pleading with my mother to control her drinking. It was raw emotion, and because I had yet to admit fully my lack of power over the problem, I expected the outburst to make an impression on my mother and get her to at least cut back. But of course it accomplished no such thing. It only made me hurt more. I had to learn the hard way that tears and accusations were no remedy for the disease I was trying so hard to get rid of.

ADDING TO THE DRINKER'S LOAD

Punishing the problem drinker has another negative affect as well: It sends him the unmistakable message that we're holding the drinking against him personally. With our ridicule and our sermons ("Why can't you behave?"), we're telling the alcoholic that he's an amoral person, someone who's misbehaving terribly or is disgustingly self-indulgent. We're sitting in judgment of his character and, not liking what we see, we hasten to let him know how poorly he's stacking up.

In essence, what we're doing is blaming him for his disease—telling him that if he were a better or stronger person, more sensitive to others—that the problem would go away. The sad truth is, the alcoholic already feels that way.

Blaming aggravates matters because it triggers two destructive processes that make it harder for the alcoholic to own up to his problem. First and foremost, it greatly exacerbates the problem drinker's already horrible feelings of guilt. Even a passing insult or snide remark ("All the other kids' parents were at the game") can add mightily to his self-disgust and his remorse about how he's ripping apart the family with his excessive drinking.

Perhaps you're thinking, "My alcoholic parent doesn't feel guilty. At least, he sure doesn't act like he does. If anything, he blames the rest of the family for his problem. He doesn't show the slightest sign of remorse about his actions." But bear in mind that this is merely his denial of the disease at work. Remember, the problem drinker is terrified about the progressive loss of control over his drinking. Deep down, he knows he is addicted, just as he knows only too well the pain he is causing his loved ones. But the fear and guilt he lives with constantly are too much for him to take, and the only way out is to deny—fiercely, with everything he can muster—that there is anything wrong at all.

It's vital to understand that the alcoholic already is punishing himself. The last thing he needs is another reminder of how horrible he is, and we must keep this in mind when we feel like striking out at our parent. Sure, the alcoholic will point fingers and rant on about being picked on or unappreciated and about how it's somebody else's fault, but all that amounts to is an overflow of self-hate pouring out of him. Feeling terribly about himself, he simply is showing the common human weakness of hiding behind a verbal attack. When things aren't right on the inside, it always shows on the outside because we take it out on others. Well, things definitely aren't right inside the alcoholic. Indeed, he's full of poison, and it's steadily eating away at him. Adding to the pain only saps him of what little self-worth he does have and leaves him that much less able to summon the internal strength to face the problem and seek help.

At all times we must keep in our heads that we're up against a disease, and that disease has never been "guilted" out of anyone. Making our parent feel terrible about himself won't move him to get help. There were times, I admit, that I felt better for having lashed out and punished my mom. It gave me a short term of relief, venting my pain with cutting remarks. But who can calculate how terrible an emotional toll that took on her, and how long it may have prevented her from getting help? Yes, it's understandable that we're so filled with powerful negative feelings. But by fully accepting the disease we're fighting, we can detach from these hurts and stifle the urge to take them out on our parent. Piling on to the alcoholic's burden does nothing but prolong the drinking. And surely that's the last thing in the world we want to do.

Helping the Alcoholic Justify His Drinking

The second way that blaming the alcoholic aggravates matters is that in the act of striking out at him, we're giving him something he desperately wants—a justification for continuing to drink.

We know how denial compels the alcoholic to look elsewhere for the real cause of his troubles. His spouse, you, your brothers and sisters, his boss—any close person in his life is solid scapegoat material. He wants to blame someone or something, and our punishing him fits the bill very nicely. "Look at how they treat me," he's thinking. "Look at how abused and unappreciated I am." Result? "Dammit, I have every right to take a drink." Unwittingly, we provide him with a handy justification.

As an example, let's say your alcoholic father has just awakened on Saturday afternoon after sleeping off a hard night's drinking. Suppose things were really bad; he barged into your room at 3 A.M. to tell you what a louse your mother is; he knocked over a lamp and smashed it to pieces; he exchanged harsh words with your mother all night long; and earlier he embarrassed you terribly by getting on the extension and speaking some drunken gibberish when you were on the phone with a friend. Let's suppose further that the disease concept is somewhat new to you, and that you're having a difficult time not taking his behavior personally. Consequently, you're feeling very much neglected and hurt, brimming over with anger and heavy, tangled thoughts as you get up to face Saturday. You're not sure whether you're hurt more by his inconsiderate, even mean, behavior, or by the way he's treating your mother, whom you found sitting alone crying over the whole mess.

Already you're frayed, but when the alcoholic finally makes his appearance—showing no remorse, offering no apologies—you snap altogether. "How can you do this to us?" you shout. "When are you going to wake up and see what you're doing? You've got Mom crying, the house is a mess, you kept us up half the night—where will it end?" And then, the clincher: "Sometimes I think I'd be better off having no father at all than having a drunk for one!" With that you storm out.

What do you suppose is going on inside the alcoholic? No matter how he reacts—angrily, docilely, apologetically—you can be sure your punishing tirade has added heavily to his inner guilt and feelings of worthlessness. But you've also given him a lot of ammunition for his self-pity. "Nobody cares about me anymore," he gets to thinking. "Nobody understands. First my wife and now my kids are turning on me. What's the use? They don't care about all that I have to put up with, about all the crap I have to go through to support this whole damn family. Things get a little out of control one night and they're jumping down my throat. They don't understand how hard I'm trying. I've got no problem with alcohol. It's just a tough time, and nobody—not one soul—cares." Overrun by such feelings, caught in a torrent of self-pity, inevitably he turns to the only place he can for comfort—the bottle. And our outburst helps him feel perfectly justified in doing so.

Evening the Score

In this fashion, we give the problem drinker an easy rationale for keeping on his same destructive course. And even worse, it can make him feel as though he's got every *right* to continue because our tongue-lashing has evened the score, so to speak, for his latest drinking binge. Thus, in the above example the alcoholic father may think, "Okay, I wasn't in too good form last night, but with that barrage I got hit with, I've certainly more than paid my penalty." To the alcoholic, groping for any justification he can find, the fact that he has taken his medicine can mean that everything is settled and he's free to resume drinking. We've talked about how the alcoholic's behavior often compares to that of a small child, and this is a good example. Like a kid who gets spanked for his wrongdoing, the problem drinker figures once the punishment has been administered, the slate is perfectly clean.

SUMMING UP

Sometimes we lose sight of the disease concept of alcoholism and, when we do, invariably the result is trying to control the alcoholic's drinking, lapsing into thinking that he is willfully trying to hurt us, and taking personally all of his repulsive drunken ways.

Failing to realize we're powerless over the disease not only makes us feel inadequate and incapable, it also prompts behavior that is very destructive to the alcoholic and only makes it more difficult for him to confront the true extent of his problem. Efforts to cut him off from his liquor supply only provoke ire and resentment, making him feel like a child-like victim whose problems are caused by an untrusting family. And the longer and harder we keep it up, the more he focuses on how terribly we're treating him—and the less he looks at the destruction his disease is wreaking on his life.

Other times we try to control the drinking by punishing him. Our hurtful feelings spill out in an avenging outburst, and we scold, nag, preach and pile on to the heaping portion of guilt he already feels. Deep down, we hope our emotional venting will show the alcoholic exactly how much hurt and damage his drinking is causing in the family, and that this painful realization will motivate him to get sober.

But this is not how the disease of alcoholism works. No display of our pain, no matter how graphic, can cure him of his compulsion to drink. No amount of guilt or shame can make him see the sad reality of his situation.

It's critical that we understand how counter-productive our controlling behavior, no matter how well-intentioned, can be. It can destroy whatever is left of the problem drinker's self-worth, leaving him even less equipped than he had been to stand up and face the problems in his life. It can feed into his self-pity, making him feel like a mistreated outcast, the downtrodden soul who everybody's picking on, and thus (in his mind) provide him with a perfectly good justification to turn to alcohol to help soothe his wounded feelings.

Finally, attempts to control the drinking by punishing the alcoholic only intensify our own feelings of hurt and abandonment. As long as we cling to the false hope that maybe we can make him see the light, that we can make a difference by showing him our pain and making him feel it too, the more shattered we will be when we find that even our most fragile and important feelings have been cast aside as if they were just another empty bottle.

There is no light we can force the alcoholic to see. There is no amount of blame or punishment that we can lay on him that will make him suddenly realize how horrible his disease has become. That's a realization the alcoholic must come to for himself. Because it's only by facing it alone that the problem drinker will acutely feel the pain the drinking is bringing on and be moved to do something about it.

Letting the Alcoholic Face the Music | 7

"My mother and I made things very easy for my father," says Diane. "We were always taking care of things he couldn't do for himself because of his drinking. If he passed out on the floor, we'd make sure we got him to bed so he'd sleep better. When he missed appointments or couldn't go to work, my mother would call in and make some excuse to cover for him. I felt like there wasn't any choice. We figured we had to take care of him or else really bad things would happen, like he would get sicker or lose his job."

Most of us figure the same thing. "When my mom's drinking got bad she started drinking earlier and earlier in the day," remembers Maggie. "Nothing ever got done. We had to do everything for her."

In my family, the situation was much the same. When my mother couldn't take care of her most basic needs and responsibilities, we would step in and do it for her. If she was too far gone to eat, we'd feed her. If she couldn't get dressed, we'd dress her. If she fell and couldn't make it to bed at night, we'd carry her there and tuck her in. When she couldn't honor some commitment or another, we'd call and make up a lie to excuse her. There was almost no end to the lengths we would go to to assist her.

THE RESCUE MENTALITY

As Diane noted, most of us feel we have no choice but to come to the aid of our alcoholic parent. What else can we do? As the drinking problem escalates, the alcoholic is less and less able to fend for himself, and if the family doesn't bail him out and keep things functioning at least at a superficial level, who will? This is the sort of attitude most of us instinctively adopt. We fall into a rescue mentality, thinking that the only way to prevent things from getting even worse is to grin and bear it, to have the whole family rally 'round and pitch in and making a family project out of limiting the damage the drinking does to the alcoholic. So when he falls, we pick him up. When he messes up, we cover for him. If he's hungry or thirsty, we better stop what we're doing and help him, because if we don't he might hurt himself, get burned, leave the stove on or provoke some other catastrophe. Sometimes we'll even try to insulate him from bad news because if he heard it he would want to drink some more and things would become more unbearable. So we might decide not to relay the angry message from his boss about his reporting late to work, or hide those mounting bills before he can see them, and hope that next month he'll be in better shape to face up to things. There's almost no limit to the actions we can take to "save" the alcoholic. We come to think of these efforts as our obligation, the way—the only way, really—we can lessen the impact of the disease. And in a sense, we might even enjoy taking care of the problem drinker. It can make us feel needed and purposeful, as though we're finally accomplishing something. Plus it seems the only thing we can do. But is it?

MISDIRECTED DEVOTION

Of course, we have only the best of intentions in our efforts to rescue and protect the alcoholic. Who wants to see a loved one in pain if we can do something to avoid it? "And besides," most of us are thinking to ourselves, "if he has any more problems or mishaps he's only going to drink more." We're helping him out so he won't be so sad, and therefore he'll have more reasons to be sober.

In a sense, we become parents—overprotective ones at that—to our own parents. Think for a moment of a rambunctious four-year-old who's fond of racing around the house at full speed. One room has a waxed wood floor that's very slippery. Naturally, the parents warn the little guy about the dangers of running on the floor. But he's too energetic to heed them. He keeps up his scurrying, and the parents are very worried about what might happen in this particular room. So they make sure they watch him carefully when he's in there. They stand by, ready to cushion his fall. Or they'll put a mat or rug down to improve the footing and make it safer if he does take a tumble. They want to do whatever they can to spare him the painful experience of falling.

And they may well succeed. They may be so vigilant that the kid doesn't get hurt. But unless they intend to hold his hand all through life, eventually he *will* fall down. Maybe it won't be on that floor; maybe it will be at the school gym or at a friend's house. But if he keeps playing speed merchant indoors, it's bound to happen. And what will happen when it does? He may bang his head, bruise a knee and get pretty shaken up. And then what will happen? He'll slow down. He will have suffered the painful consequences of his racing, and he'll have thus learned a lesson.

Pain and/or unpleasantness can greatly motivate us to change. It's a self-correcting instinct we have, and without it life would be a mess. If something hurts and there's some action we can take to reduce or stop it, we take it. I recall an episode when I was seven and an older friend dared me to throw a rock into a bush covered with yellow jackets. I said no, but he kept on goading me. Finally, I said the heck with it, and fired a rock right into the middle of the bush. Seconds later, I was racing home to Mom, tears streaming down my cheeks and a bee stinger in my forehead. But I can tell you this much: It was the last time I ever threw a rock into a bush full of bees.

Learning lessons is an integral part of living and growing. And often the way we learn is by, like our hyperactive little kid, taking a tumble, feeling a hurt and resolving to do something to stop it from happening again. Of course this isn't to say we should never protect or come to the aid of our loved ones; clearly, we're not going to let someone walk in the path of an oncoming car so he or she can learn a lesson that such behavior is dangerous. But when the consequences are not potentially fatal, when they're more likely to be frustration, discomfort, pain, etc., we must try to check the urge continually to insulate people from them. Ultimately, we all must be responsible for our own actions. To jump in and rescue is to rob a person—especially an alcoholic—of any motivation to change.

THE HIGH COST OF ENABLING

So even though we mean well, we do the alcoholic a major disservice by rescuing him, a practice that commonly is referred to as enabling, in the sense that in our overprotective zeal we are enabling the alcoholic to continue drinking without ever having to face fully the damaging fallout of his disease.

Our parents are adults. They must be expected to look after themselves and take care of their own needs. If, because of excessive drinking, your parent is failing in those ways, then the most constructive thing you can do is to allow him to confront the consequences of the drinking. Cold-hearted as it sounds and as hard as this can be, not rushing to the problem drinker's rescue is the greatest act of love we can give him.

I could not accept this at first. I heard other kids talking about it at Alateen meetings, but it made no sense to me that my mother would in any way benefit from having to sleep on the floor, go a whole day without food or have to face a neighbor herself after failing to keep a commitment. I wanted to get in there and smooth everything over and make her life as serene and normal as possible. Keep her from sinking too low, and things eventually will straighten out—that was my thinking.

But the thinking was faulty, and gradually, as I sat with the idea that enabling is damaging to the problem drinker, I had to admit that throughout the period of all my rescuing efforts, the problem had only gotten worse. Eventually I had to face it: My devoted efforts to protect and insulate only made it easier for my mother to continue her drinking. This was the realization that compelled me to change my ways, not only because I wasn't making things any better, but because I was without doubt making them worse.

Perhaps you, too, are having trouble accepting that your enabling can actually intensify the drinking problem. Granted, bailing out the alcoholic just doesn't seem to be the sort of thing that could make the compulsion worse. But when we take into account the problem drinker's denial, how afraid he is of what's happening to him and how desperately he wants not to face the truth, it begins to make sense. Because what are we really doing when we enable the alcoholic? We're taking actions that allow him to continue avoiding the truth. We're helping him minimize the impact drinking is having on his life. We're shielding him from the damage—and eliminating the chance that he'll come to see that alcohol is ruining his life.

An alcoholic's denial is slow to die. He clings to it as long as he can because he can't fathom living without having alcohol to numb the pain. Only when the problem drinker comes face to face with the destruction the disease is causing will the denial be overpowered. And only by letting go of our rescuer role can we help that to happen. You'll recall at the outset how we talked of the problem drinker using alcohol as an escape from deep psychological pain—anxiety, depression, guilt, low self-esteem, etc. It is only when the pain caused by the drinking exceeds the pain that they're trying to escape that most alcoholics will bottom out and, in the depths of their despair, realize that the disease is raging out of control and that they need to do something about it. It is a humbling and painful experience for the alcoholic, and it's no picnic for us either—watching someone we love hit what people involved with alcoholism often call "rock bottom." But it is the starting point for recovery, and as such, a tremendous source of hope for brighter days ahead.

Letting go of our enabling ways is as hard as anything we'll ever have to do. We want so badly to make things better, but we need to keep reminding ourselves that not rescuing our parent *is* the way to make things better. To get well, the alcoholic must take his own medicine, and that means that he has to face the damage his addiction is causing. For us in the family, that means we don't cushion the blows. It means we don't call and offer an excuse after Dad is so hung over he oversleeps and misses the important meeting with the vice-president. It means we don't call and apologize ("Sorry, Bob just wasn't himself last night") when the alcoholic has a drunken tantrum at a neighbor's house. It means we don't sit up with him half the night because he's lonely and wants us to, and because we think it'll make him feel better and maybe drink less tomorrow. It means we don't feed him, bathe him, try sobering him up, put him to bed or assume any other of his most basic responsibilities. If and when you get thinking that this seems cold and cruel, bear in mind that by interfering less we're helping him more—much more. By not cleaning up all the alcohol-related debris in his life, we're helping to push him in the only healthy direction there is—toward a realization that drinking is causing him big problems and that he has to do something about it.

BRACING FOR A GUILT TRIP

As we learn to let go of rescuing, often we will be targets for the alcoholic's hostility and/or guilt. The reason the drinker responds this way could not be clearer: he liked it better—and his life was easier—when we took care of everything for him. He doesn't want anything to change. And why would he? No matter what trouble he worked himself into, somehow we would step in and get him out of it. So when we begin stopping our enabling, we have to be prepared for an onslaught.

I remember very vividly my mother's reaction when I first let go of enabling. One step I took was to stop putting myself on 24-hour call to take care of her physical and emotional needs. One Friday night I announced that I was going out with friends. Nobody else was home. "Good, leave your mother home all by herself and go out and have a great time," she sneered. Her guilt-peddling worked at first. The tape began running through my head: "What kind of son am I? Maybe I should stay with her; maybe she'd feel better and drink less, and we'd have a better day tomorrow." But, fortunately, I was able to get some right thinking back pretty quickly. "I can't control her drinking," I reminded myself. "Staying home and holding her hand all night has never done any good before, has it? I can't spend my life catering to her whims. Her drinking has nothing to do with my wanting to go out and have a little fun. I am not a bad son for doing something for myself." I wasn't able instantly to stop feeling conflicted about it; these things aren't so tidy as that. But I did go out that night, and by keeping in mind the basic ideas we've talked about in this book, my inner turmoil gradually quieted.

There's almost no end to the ways the problem drinker may try to manipulate us into continuing our enabling ways. Tears, anger, self-pity, a sulking silence—any of these ploys might be used if the alcoholic thinks it might weaken our resolve and get us back to rescuing. You may hear the old refrain, "If you loved me you'd help me." You may even get a dose of blackmail; to get her way, my mom frequently would try it on me, usually saying something like, "If you leave me, I'm going to drive to a bar." Or, "If you won't do such and such, I'm going to call up your friends and let them know what a drunk you've got for a mother." Riddled with the disease, the alcoholic will push any button he thinks will get to us—and help him get his way. Often he will stop at nothing. More than once my mother threatened suicide if I didn't comply with her wishes. "If you don't take care of me I'm going to kill myself," she said.

Obviously this is brutal stuff to hear. Equally obvious is that it puts us in an excruciating spot: Do we stick to our guns and not rescue the problem drinker, at the risk of him falling and hurting himself, spilling a drink or getting sick on the new couch? At the risk of him embarrassing himself terribly, perhaps by going outside in his pajamas or visiting neighbors and demanding a drink? At the risk of him getting behind the wheel and cracking up the car and getting hurt? Even at the risk of him trying to kill himself?

Such situations confront us with almost impossible choices. There is no right course of action for us that holds true in every instance. But we can say this much: Protecting the alcoholic from the damage of his drinking is counter-productive and will only make the problem worse. Enabling can be an insidious habit; we begin just helping the alcoholic in little ways—making sure he's eating right or that he looks presentable—but almost always it escalates to bigger ways. Before long we're doing all we can to ensure he hangs on to his job, stays out of debt, doesn't embarrass himself or the family—the list goes on and on. Eventually we get to a point where we become almost full-time enablers and rescuers, at the expense of just about everything that's important in our own lives. Jeanine put it this way:

> It's so frustrating. I feel trapped, like I have to do everything for her. I'm the one in the family that my mother really leans on, and if I'm not there I don't know what would happen. I'm afraid when I'm not there. What's she doing? How much is she drinking? Can she take care of herself? Next year I'm going off to college, and I'm already worried about what will happen then.

Once we get hooked into rescuing, it can be very hard to get unhooked. For many of us, it feels as though if we weren't around to fix things, the alcoholic, or the whole family, would self-destruct. What we need to keep in mind is that total self-sacrifice is extremely unhealthy. We must remember that all the devotion on earth cannot rid the alcoholic of the disease; it's like using a Band-Aid on a gaping wound. We cannot allow our own lives to come to a standstill. Not only is it healthy for us, it's our *right* to take care of our own needs and pursue our own interests. Certainly, unpleasant and destructive things will occur as we stop rescuing. Maybe that new couch will get ruined by the careless drunk. Maybe the alcoholic will get in a fight with a neighbor, crack up the car, even lose his job. The damage of alcoholism can take a multitude of forms, many of them horrible. But we need to have faith that in allowing these terrible things to occur, by not intervening, we're helping the alcoholic confront the true magnitude of his disease. There is pain along the way, but in exchange for it we're dramatically increasing the chance that the alcoholic will own up to his problem and seek treatment. And isn't that a whole lot better than the status quo, than our vainly trying to hold things together as things get steadily worse?

WHEN ACTION NEEDS TO BE TAKEN

Our discussion here should not be taken to mean that we should never rescue the alcoholic, regardless of circumstances. In an occasional extreme case, we may have to do something to save the alcoholic from serious injury or even death. In such instances we must either rely on our own instincts, or even better, talk to a trusted friend or counselor. For example, I never took my mother's suicide threats seriously. I watched over her very carefully the first few times the threats were made. And I worried plenty. But as I heard it more often, something deep inside let me know this was only a tactic to make me continue enabling her.

This in no way means that every suicide threat from an alcoholic is idle. If you're hearing it for the first time or you have the slightest reason to believe the alcoholic might try it, immediately get in touch with your sober parent, a suicide hotline (usually listed in the white pages), a family doctor, counselor, an aunt or uncle—anyone you think might be able to provide instant guidance and help. See the Appendix for more details on handling crisis situations involving the alcoholic.

A PARTING THOUGHT

Letting go of enabling is an important step in shaking free of the shackles of the disease, and allowing us to move our lives forward. We know that when you live with this disease long enough, it's easy—dangerously so—to focus only on the alcoholic and his ongoing battle with the bottle. What we need to do, to borrow a slogan from Alateen and Al-Anon, is to "keep the focus on ourselves." We are the masters of our own fate; we're the ones who have the responsibility to take care of ourselves and our needs. This isn't being selfish, it's being realistic.

Many people—and I was one of them—equate loving with enabling. They feel that not coming to the alcoholic's rescue is an act of abandonment. And as we've noted, the alcoholic often will underscore that sense, piling on the guilt to keep that enabling coming.

But loving and enabling are not the same. We can choose not to enable the problem drinker and still love him as much as the greatest enabler. Indeed, letting go of our rescue efforts is the most loving way we can treat him. Because only by allowing him to see and feel tte full effects of his disease will he be motivated to seek help. It's also among the most loving things we can do for ourselves, for it's our responsibility—nobody else's—to attend to our own basic needs. Doing things for others, helping people in distress, is kind and even noble. But to do so to an extent where we're solving others' problems, assuming their responsibilities and protecting them from themselves, is destructive to everyone involved. It is sacrifice to the point of self-denial.

We need to be extremely careful about not letting the

bottle become the centerpiece of our existence. We need to remember at all times that we have our own lives to live. By realizing that ultimately we have no power over the disease, and understanding that no amount of protecting and rescuing can ever lead the alcoholic to find the help he needs, we can free ourselves to pursue things that will help us grow, despite the stagnation we see around us.

I'm reminded of an episode that occurred when I first stopped taking care of my mother's every need. She saw I was getting ready to go out. She was pretty far gone. "Where are you going?" she demanded.

"I'm going to a meeting."

"What kind of meeting?"

I hesitated. "An Alateen meeting." She hit the roof, ranting about how I had no right to talk to other people about our family affairs, and about how it was mean—and an act of betrayal—for me even to consider discussing the effect her drinking had on me. She also laid on the guilt. "I need you here tonight," she sobbed. "Please, please, stay with me. You can help me. You can save me. Oh, please don't leave me here alone."

I went to the meeting and I was glad I did. I shared some of my feelings and heard a lot of things that helped clear my head, ease my load, and put the drinking in perspective. Misery loves company, the old saying goes, and as much as I love my mother, love does not require us to be miserable.

Walking out of the house that night wasn't easy. In fact, it was one of the hardest things I've ever had to do. But it was good—even necessary —for me. Once I got to the meeting, I never gave it one regretful thought. And I got the added bonus of knowing that maybe, without me around to feed her, protect her, steady her on her feet and make sure things didn't get out of hand, my mother got a lot more of a clue as to the disease that was raging inside her—a clue which eventually contributed to her realizing that for her to put her life back together, sobriety was the only answer.

Giving the Alcoholic
Loving Support | 8

We've looked at why we must not step in and take care of the things the problem drinker is expected to do for himself. We've discussed the importance of not trying to control the disease and how to stop obsessing about it. We've also looked at the importance of detaching from the alcoholism—understanding that the pain it causes is not directed at us personally and trying to limit our emotional hurt by realizing that the alcoholic's enormous unhappiness—his guilt, his self-loathing—prompts him to project it onto those closest to him.

Given these approaches to the problem, you may be thinking that what we're really recommending is to have as little to do as possible with the problem drinker—at least until his disease is under control. And undoubtedly such complete withdrawal would often seem to be the most attractive alternative. I went through a phase when I was living at home in body only. I stayed in my room as much as possible, tried hard to ignore the ever-darkening gloom I was surrounded by, and whether my mother was drunk or sober, had as little interaction with her as I could. At least I wasn't enabling all over the place, as I used to, so in that sense my pulling back was constructive. But in a larger sense it was not constructive at all. And though my reaction was understandable, I soon learned that I'd missed the point.

DETACHING WITH LOVE

Detachment is not about closing the alcoholic out of our lives or making a full-fledged flight from the problems in our home. Nor is it about moping around in a stony silence. Such behavior can be even more self-defeating than blaming or enabling the alcoholic. Because when we examine it closely, what is our retreat and silence other than just another, albeit more subtle, way of punishing our alcoholic parent? What are we doing except lashing him with our wordlessness? Though unstated, our message is unmistakable: You are a drunk, and because of that I don't want anything to do with you. I'm not even going to talk to you. You have forfeited your right to be a part of my life.

Why is this approach so damaging? Much as with the other ways of punishing the drinker, it only feeds into the whopping guilt and self-disgust he already feels, further weakening him and giving him that much more pain to escape from. But it delivers the blow with ferocious force, because by ignoring him we're in effect telling him he's not only unlovable, but not even worth arguing with, nagging or scolding.

True detachment, on the other hand, is a healthy, loving way of treating the alcoholic. It's a way of emotionally distancing ourselves from the ravages of the disease, without emotionally distancing ourselves from the loved one who is suffering from it. Is it hard to achieve? You bet. Often it may seem nearly impossible. Suppose it's the day after a night-long drunken rage in which your parent did everything he could think of to hurt you. Maybe you're sensitive about your weight, and he made jokes about what a tub you are. Maybe he belittled your friends, blamed you for his desire to drink or called you stupid for not doing better in school. One young person I talked with told of how her father, when under the influence, invariably would bring up the fact that she had had an abortion, which by far was the most painful experience of her life. As we've noted, because they're suffering so much inner unhappiness themselves, most alcoholics are great button-pushers who will find ways to spill some of the negativity onto their loved ones.

In the face of such barrages, remaining detached may seem out of the question. It's difficult, but it can be done. And for things to get better and for us to feel better, it must be done. The key, as we've seen time and again, is gaining a clear understanding of the disease, and of how and why the alcoholic's compulsion to drink makes him behave in so many ugly, hurtful ways.

CAN WE EVER CONFRONT THE ALCOHOLIC?

Sometimes we may feel we're deluged with don'ts when dealing with our alcoholic parent. Don't blame, nag or scold him; don't accuse him or add to his guilt; don't preach to him about how he should reform, but don't give him the cold shoulder either. Perhaps you're wondering, are there any dos? Are there healthy ways of communicating with the alcoholic? Is there any place at all for our painful feelings about what the disease is doing to us?

The answers are yes, yes and yes. The reason behind the don'ts has nothing to do with stifling our feelings and turning ourselves into martyrs who never complain and just keep on getting hurt. Rather, it has to do with relating to the problem drinker in a way that's constructive for all concerned.

There's nothing in the least wrong with letting our parent know we're worried about his drinking and that it is creating difficulties for us. Indeed, an enormous amount of good can come of it, provided you approach the talk in a straightforward, non-accusatory, non-judgmental manner.

Keep the focus on your feelings, and not on what he is doing to you. Hard as it may be to believe in view of the numbing qualities of liquor, alcoholics are extremely sensitive people. And they are especially sensitive when it comes to feeling guilt and blame. If the drinker senses that our talking with him is motivated by our wanting to get back at him by making him feel badly, chances are he will become angry, sullen or slip deeper into his self-pity, and the conversation will do nothing, except possibly start a fight.

But the alcoholic will sense just as readily when we're motivated by love and compassion, when we confront him with a deep concern for his well-being. He will be more receptive to what we're saying, even if he doesn't display it openly, and he'll also be far less likely to become defensive. We need to remember: If we don't attack, he won't feel the need to defend—to make excuses or counter-attack. And that will leave us with dramatically increased chances for truly getting our point across. So instead of saying "You're turning everybody into a nervous wreck," we want to say, "I'm very worried about your drinking." Instead of saying, "You're a liar! You broke your promise to go shopping with me last Saturday," we want to say, "I was hurt when we didn't get to spend the day together the way we'd planned." Instead of, "Keep this up and you're going to get fired, and then where will we be?", say, "I get upset when you miss so much time from work." Instead of, "You make me sick the way you treat Mom," say, "I get all tense when I see you and Mom fighting over your drinking." Instead of, "How could you pass out on the floor when you knew I was bringing friends over?" say, "I felt embarrassed and angry when I brought my friends over and you were passed out. I sent them home because I was afraid of what might happen when you woke up."

The differences between stating our feelings and making an accusation sometimes can be very subtle; indeed, reading the above examples quickly, you might be hard-pressed to discern any difference at all. But there is a difference and, particularly to the alcoholic, it's a very big one. We need to keep our all-important guidepost of detachment foremost in mind when we're going to share our feelings with our alcoholic parent. For it's only with a detached view of the situation that we'll be able to put the emphasis where it belongs—on our feelings and concerns and the facts of how alcohol is damaging everyone's life—and not lapse into an accusatory tirade.

A BRIEF LOOK AT INTERVENTION

Confronting the alcoholic in this studiously non-judgmental way is regarded as such an effective approach that it has become incorporated into a widely practiced therapy known as intervention. Earlier we looked at how the alcoholic has to hit rock bottom—become fully and painfully aware of the mess his drinking is causing—before he can be truly ready to get help. A recently developed concept, intervention is an alternative to having the problem drinker bottom out. In intervention, those closest to the alcoholic (his family and sometimes his best friends and/or co-workers) work with a trained counselor (usually the counselors are affiliated with alcohol rehabilitation centers) and compile specific, straightforward and absolutely factual and non-judging examples of how alcohol is interfering with family life. The counselor assists the family in eliminating all traces of blaming, scolding and sermonizing from the examples (so instead of, "It was really disgusting when you got so bombed last Thursday that you came home and got sick all over my $500 carpet," the drinker's spouse might say simply, "You vomited all over the new carpet last Thursday"). If there are any overtones of hostility, the confrontation can crumble into just another family shouting match. When it's done properly, however, when the family is carefully counseled so that all that comes up is a firm but emotionally detached rundown of many of the ugly episodes the drinker either has forgotten or wants to forget, the intervention can jolt the alcoholic into an acute awareness of just how bad things are getting.

PICKING THE RIGHT TIME TO TALK

We have just one more don't to dispense with: Don't talk about your feelings with the alcoholic while he's under the influence. It's an exercise in futility that will yield only increased frustration and anger on your part. With the alcoholic's impaired mental state, it's practically impossible for a conversation to be reasonable and constructive.

The best course of action while your parent is drinking is to avoid as many confrontations as possible. I know this is often easier said than done; frequently my mother would become extremely belligerent while drinking, and go out of her way to pick a fight. She often wanted a shouting match, and sometimes she got it. But we need to remember that arguing with a drunk can be nothing but unpleasant; nothing will be resolved and it will likely go on for a long time. Even if your parent is goading you or saying nasty things, try to detach and respond—if a response is demanded—by saying something simple and direct, such as, "I really don't feel like getting into that now." Or, "I'm sorry you feel that way." The less tangled up you get, the better off you'll be. Just keep working on your detachment; keep the following mental tape handy and run it through your head often: "My parent has a disease; this is not his true self and what he's saying are not his true feelings."

THE DAY AFTER

My mother's behavior when she came off a drinking bout varied widely. Sometimes she would be remorseful and profusely apologetic. Other times she would seem every bit as angry as she had been while under the influence. At still other times she was sullen and almost vacant, as though she wasn't even there.

The unpredictability of her sober manner made things difficult for me. It was just another situation in which I didn't know what to expect. But no matter what the alcoholic is like when sober, we have to focus on being positive and letting go of blame.

Suppose you come home from school all pumped up one day because you've won an award for your schoolwork. Naturally you're excited about sharing the good news with your parents. You arrive at home to find your alcoholic mother, say, in a foul mood and well on her way to drunkenness. She shows little interest in your accomplishment. In fact, later on in the evening she says acidly, "It's about time you did something. Your brother won four of those awards."

Now it's the following day and your mother is sober. How do you treat her? Still hurting from her nastiness of the night before, do you walk past her without a word? Do you snap back with a revengeful comment, maybe, "If you weren't drunk all the time, maybe I could win more awards"?

Certainly there's a powerful impulse to get back at her. And certainly you have every right to be hurt that a significant achievement was received only with a snide remark. Still, getting even is both unfair and destructive.

We have to devote ourselves fully to practicing detachment, not only during the difficult drunken times, but the sober times as well. Indeed, we could make a good case for detachment being even more important when our alcoholic parent is sober, because that's when he's most vulnerable and overflowing with negative feelings about himself and his actions. And that's when our efforts to be supportive, compassionate and loving can do the most good.

Going back to our example, let's say your mom spots the letter of congratulations from the principal. "What's this for?" she says, obviously suffering a blackout from your discussion of the night before. With your detached view, with full knowledge that your mother has a disease and that she did not mean to hurt you with last night's actions, you might say, with extreme non-judgment, "That's for the award I won in English class. We talked about it last night but I guess you don't remember. The school is having an award banquet next Tuesday; do you think you'll be able to make it?"

We do not have to fawn over our alcoholic parent, nor

must we feel obliged to be all sweetness so he might feel better about himself. What we do need to do, however, is to treat him with the respect due him. We need to involve him in our lives as much as we can, given the limits created by his illness. Maybe you're suffering a slight mental slip and you're thinking, "Why should I treat him with respect? He doesn't treat me that way." Or, "He shows me every time he gets drunk that he doesn't care, so why should I involve him in anything?" But such thoughts aren't recognizing your parent's illness. We wouldn't treat our parent with disrespect if he suffered from tuberculosis. Nor should we do so because he suffers from a drinking problem.

We need to work hard at not locking our parent out of our lives because we're wrongfully holding a grudge from his drinking. We have to be careful not to discount him entirely just because he happens to have a drinking problem. I know, for instance, that I probably went several years without asking my mother for advice or counseling on a particular problem. I'd find somebody else because she either wouldn't care or wouldn't have anything to say. Even though I wasn't consciously punishing her with this, I nonetheless was drawing back from her and adding to her feelings of being unneeded and unloved. Keep in mind that even with his disease, there are many times our drinking parent is ready, even eager, to help us out. The smallest step to involve your parent—asking for help on a school project, seeing if he'd like to attend the new movie in town, inquiring about what colleges he thinks would be best for you—can mean far more to him than you might ever suspect.

We also need to keep in mind that treating our parent in this way is the mature and right thing to do, no matter how he might respond. Sometimes our overtures will be ridiculed or fall on deaf ears. Sometimes our parent might even try to provoke an argument. "Why are you asking me about colleges all of a sudden when you ignored me before when I tried talking with you?" Try your best not to get hooked into a dispute. It can only do harm, because when we start getting angry invariably detachment is one of the first things to fly out the window, and the next thing we know we're back into a blaming and nagging routine. With practice, we can develop responses that will help avoid flare-ups, even when our parent's disease seems intent on spreading its poison and unhappiness all over us. "Well, I guess I wasn't ready to talk about colleges then. But I really would like to hear your suggestions now." We have no guarantees that our respectful, caring manner will yield any immediate good. The alcoholic might seem disinterested or angry in spite of our best efforts. With no control over his reactions, we can still take comfort that regardless of what he says or does, we've communicated with him in a manner that's healthy for all concerned.

We also can take comfort in knowing the negative things we haven't done: We *haven't* given him any cause to feel worse about himself; cornered him into making a promise—one he cannot keep—to stay off the sauce; or given him reasons to escape back to the bottle. Instead, in treating him with basic courtesy and kindness—quite likely, the way we'd treat him if a drinking problem never had surfaced—we've injected hope and light into an environment usually marked by gloom.

AN INCENTIVE TO SEEK HELP

We discussed in the previous chapter how allowing the problem drinker to confront the painful results of his drinking can give him a powerful motivation to do something about his disease. That motivation can also get a big boost from our treating him with the support and compassion that spring from our loving detachment. Why? Because rather than belittling him and sapping him of inner strength, our actions encourage and fortify him. They leave him with a better feeling about himself, and that in turn leaves him far better equipped to begin dealing with his disease. They will not make him go running immediately to an Alcoholics Anonymous meeting; but over time, little by little, our healthy approach to him, our efforts to detach from his disease but still give him the love and support he so sorely needs (and cannot give himself), will give him strength to draw on.

And he will need it. Admitting the disease and seeking treatment takes a lot of strength and courage. Before he can take one step toward recovery, he needs to feel that his life is worth making the long, arduous journey back to health. The easiest thing to do by far for the alcoholic is to keep right on drinking, to wallow in self-pity and convince himself there's nothing to salvage out of life anyway. And that's where our care and compassion for him come in. Our actions prove to him that there in fact *is* a great deal to salvage. He may not think he's worth saving, but our actions are telling him otherwise, and that support can make all the difference. They show that we still love him, that we're standing by him in spite of his terrible illness. Even when these feelings aren't made explicit, the alcoholic senses our support, and that's only good. In a very basic way, our kindness and respect give him more reason to seek treatment. "Look at what a wonderful family I have," the alcoholic might say to himself. "Look at all the reasons I have to get better." Seeing that we're still there for him can be a powerful experience; after all, his feelings of worthlessness are so deep-seated that it can positively lift the weight of the world from him when he recognizes that others think he's worth quite a bit.

The alcoholic may never express this in words. He may not be an instant fountain of gratitude the moment he decides he must get help. But we can be assured that what we're doing is right even if we don't hear it from him. It's right because in working on ourselves to counter the effects of the family illness, we've resisted getting swept up by the disease's rampant negativity. We're neither feeding his insatiable appetite for guilt and self-loathing, nor blaming him and thus giving him reason to head for a drink. Rather, we've taken the huge step of loving him in a detached way—caring for him and respecting him, even as we go on being repulsed by his disease. You can bet the ranch and record collection that he notices the difference, and that it's giving him a lot of extra strength and motivation to take a long, hard look at what his drinking is doing to him.

Only he can make the decision to stop drinking. But we can help and, with an enlightened approach in relating to the alcoholic, that help can sometimes give our parent the final push he needs to realize there are a lot of great things to live for—and just as many to stop drinking for.

When Your Parent
Gets Sober | 9

You're probably familiar with the old saying, "You can lead a horse to water, but you can't make him drink." It may be 110 degrees in the shade and we may *know* water would be the best thing for him, but when it gets right down to it, what can we do?

We face a similar predicament in dealing with the alcoholic. We know the drinking problem is ruining his life and that it's critical for his well-being that he stop. In the last two chapters we've discussed how we can spur him toward that realization, first by allowing him to face the gravity of the disease and, second, by treating him with respect and support and thus showing him there's a lot to get sober for. But as with the horse, the decision actually to take the positive action ultimately rests with the alcoholic alone.

What happens when the all-important—and long-awaited—step is taken? How might it affect us? How will things change? Let's look at these and other questions surrounding the treatment of alcoholism.

FINDING THE WAY

In most instances the drying out process begins with detoxification, a Latin word that literally means "undoing poison," which indeed is what the alcoholic is accomplishing. An extended period of heavy drinking invariably takes a heavy toll on the drinker's overall physical condition. He may be suffering from damage to the liver, heart, stomach, pancreas, have severe nutritional deficiencies and find himself with an impaired ability to reason and remember. By the time he seeks treatment, he almost certainly is also physically addicted to alcohol, meaning that he's going to experience withdrawal symptoms as he rids his body of the poison it has become so dependent on. Headaches, nausea, abdominal cramps, and particularly extreme shakiness, hallucinations and convulsions, can make withdrawal a painful and terrifying ordeal. For these reasons alcoholics are strongly urged to undergo detoxification in a hospital or an alcohol rehabilitation center with a detox (as it's widely known) program. The process usually takes five to seven days, depending on the extent of the addiction. Problem drinkers who also are addicted to other drugs (typically tranquilizers, anti-depressants or other pills) will require extra time to purge their bodies.

Even apart from the obvious medical necessity, a detox program (whether in a hospital or rehabilitation center) also helps by removing the alcoholic from his drinking environment—all the familiar haunts and connections which, particularly in the beginning, he associates with drinking. And further, the medical setting helps him realize that he has a disease. Humbled, defeated and severely run down from their abuse, alcoholics at this point tend to feel enormous guilt and self-disgust about being in such a state. They're repulsed by their condition and loathe themselves for getting into it. But in receiving medical treatment for their physical addiction, alcoholics can begin accepting that they did not sink to such a state just because they were lushes who liked to have a good time, but because they acquired a disease that brought on a compulsive need to use alcohol as a means of escape.

Following the detox period many alcoholics go to a rehabilitation center, which provides intensive treatment and education about the disease of alcoholism, as well as about how the newly sober alcoholic must learn to cope with his life and problems without his escape hatch, and how he needs to change his basic attitudes and behavior patterns for his sobriety to endure. Most rehabilitation programs last about four weeks.

The therapy, support and guidance the alcoholic receives in a rehab center often can provide him with a solid foundation on which to build an alcohol-free life. However, because this help is dispensed in a highly sheltered environment, where everybody's patting the ex-drinker on the back, assuring him he can do it, cautioning him of the perils of his disease and where he's free of day-to-day pressures and problems, the alcoholic sometimes can find it a difficult transition when he returns to his own private world. Outside the rehab, for instance, your parent might have to deal with mounting bills that were neglected during the drinking. Or he may face the pressure of finding a new job, or proving himself all over again if he still has his old one. Sometimes your parent may even be worried about what will happen when he sees his old drinking buddies, or passes the gin mill he always used to hit on the way home. Nothing we can say or do can make this adjustment an easy one. We should just try to keep in mind that it is a hard time for our parent, understand what he's experiencing if he doesn't seem to be himself and offer him as much support and compassion as we can.

ANTABUSE

Sometimes during early sobriety alcoholics are prescribed a drug called Antabuse. Most experts feel strongly that sobriety should be achieved without tranquilizers or mood-altering drugs such as antidepressants, reasoning that alcoholics will be prone to getting addicted to them just as they did to alcohol. Antabuse, however, does not change one's mood. It is a drug that simply provokes strong and unpleasant reactions when mixed with alcohol. Severe headaches, nausea, vomiting, breathing trouble—all of these may be experienced when the two drugs are mixed. Reactions commence within five to 10 minutes of alcohol intake, and can last from 30 minutes to several hours, depending on how much alcohol is consumed.

Always dispensed with the alcoholic's full knowledge, Antabuse is used as a supplement to customary treatment, in which the focus is on getting at the underlying problems and attitudes that played a significant role in the onset of the disease. Because it provokes such disagreeable side-effects, it can be a powerful incentive to stay away from alcohol, but Antabuse by itself should not be considered a complete and lasting treatment for the disease.

ONE DAY AT A TIME

A key fact to be aware of is that recovering from the disease is not like flicking a switch; problem drinkers do not simply decide that alcohol has gotten the better of them and snap right back to health. There's no medicine that provides an instant cure and no therapy that can assure a full and speedy recovery. Indeed, most experts in the field agree that the disease cannot be cured in the traditional medical sense; it can be effectively treated and the drinking can stop, but the disease itself, though in remission, always remains in the alcoholic.

For this reason, alcoholics are cautioned about thinking, after several months or years of not drinking, that they have the disease licked. They can stay sober and halt the compulsion to drink, but the complex web of underlying factors that spawned the alcohol dependency is still there. And because it's there, an alcoholic can never really be said to be out of the woods, so to speak. The disease can flare up again, and the urge to drink can resurface and overpower his desire to stop it—if the alcoholic is not fully committed to getting sober, or fully convinced that he has no power over the way he consumes alcohol. Because the disease requires constant vigilance, one of the cornerstones of Alcoholics Anonymous, a worldwide self-help organization devoted to helping people with drinking problems get sober and stay sober, is to choose not to drink "one day at a time." A.A. urges its members not to worry about whether they'll be sober five years or five months or even five days from now. Rather, the focus has to be on the present, on never losing sight of the perils of the disease and on working, day by day, to overcome problem areas and thus pave the way for a richer, healthier life.

STARTS AND STOPS

The road to sobriety can take many different turns. For some the going is fairly smooth and uninterrupted, like a wide, well-paved highway. For others it may seem perfectly navigable, until all of a sudden they hit a detour—and lose the way for a time. And then there are those for whom it seems like a twisting, backwoods path, one that they struggle to follow in spite of the hazards they encounter at nearly every turn.

It's important to realize that frequently there are stops and starts in the alcoholic's recovery. When an alcoholic suffers a relapse and resumes drinking, it's commonly known as a slip. Slips can occur for any number of reasons, all of which are extremely difficult for us to understand or predict, since it's not possible for us to have any idea of the intensity of the internal pressures the alcoholic may feel to drink. Some slips may come about because the alcoholic has not fully admitted that he cannot control his drinking to any degree. This may be hard for us to believe since we've watched, often for years, the horrors caused by alcohol, but we can never lose sight of the extraordinary power of the disease's denial. It might happen, for instance, that the alcoholic will stop for a period and decide that he's proven to everyone that he *can* control his drinking, and therefore can safely resume it.* As usual, the drinker will be extremely defensive about any family efforts to warn him against taking a drink. "Get off my back," he might say. "Your getting on me is what caused the trouble to begin with." Or he might point to the irrefutable evidence that he had, in fact, controlled it for the sober time, and thus was not to be lumped with the alcoholics of the world. But in discounting the disease's progression, he fails to realize that the alcoholism will rapidly retake control over his life and take him down the same ruinous road. He also fails to understand that his temporary abstinence does not mean he isn't alcoholic. Plenty of drinkers stop temporarily; but the disease remains, and its capability to wreak havoc on his life is never further away than the bottle.

This misplaced confidence in his ability to drink normally can occur after a few weeks, a few months or even a few years of sobriety. Usually it hits with crushing force on those of us in the family, who've waited and hoped so long and hard for better times. "My father had a slip after three years," recalls Diane. "And that was after going to a rehabilitation place and going to A.A. meetings regularly. I just couldn't believe it. It really made me angry because it seemed so stupid. It was like he was telling us all over again that drinking was more important to him than my mother and me." Her father showed absolutely no control right from the moment he resumed, Diane said. The drinking was heavier than ever before. "Things had never been worse," she said. Eventually her father bottomed out again, went back to A.A., got sober and has stayed sober for close to 10 years. Now he seems fully committed to sobriety, but he hastens to add, "I'm choosing not to drink a day at a time."

---

* A small minority of professionals in the field believes that in time it is possible for a small percentage of alcoholics to resume social drinking after being treated for the disease. Having always maintained that total abstinence is essential for complete recovery, Alcoholics Anonymous and many other groups hotly dispute this contention. For purposes of our discussion, we'll stick with the majority opinion, which would seem to have an overwhelming weight of evidence on its side—evidence that strongly suggests that an alcoholic can recover fully only by abstaining from drinking altogether.

The point is that we have no guarantees when it comes to recovery. Though grateful and respectful of her father's current sobriety, Diane seemed to have good reason to believe that alcoholism was out of her life years ago—and then her father suffered his slip. This does not mean that we need to live in constant fear no matter how long our parents may be sober. All it means is that for us, too, life with alcoholism needs to be taken one day at a time. Once sober, there's a very good chance your parent will stay sober. A.A. claims a recovery rate of about 75 percent and has helped thousands and thousands of alcoholics, many seemingly as hopeless as could be, rebuild their lives. But we shouldn't take sobriety for granted. Recovery from alcoholism is a process, because we're not just talking about a physical disease, but an emotional and psychological one as well. In essence, a recovering alcoholic is learning to live all over again. He's learning to face stresses, conflicts and problems without using alcohol as an escape. He's working to rebuild himself so that he is able to cope with daily pressures and setbacks.

We need to remember that for as long as he has been drinking, the alcoholic's only coping mechanism was the bottle. Feeling weak and inadequate and incapable of handling his life alone, he turned to alcohol to see him through. And as he starts letting go, he still has deep-seated doubts about whether he has the strength to make it without his crutch. He confronts many stiff challenges to his sobriety in the course of daily living. Slips do not result just from overconfidence about one's ability to handle liquor; they also can occur when the alcoholic is confronted by a difficult burden or problem, even a tense situation. At such trying times his disease, dormant but still inside him, is saying, "Go get a drink. Alcohol will make you feel better. You'll be more relaxed. Things will be more manageable. You don't need to get drunk. Just a drink—one drink—that's all you need to make everything better." He has to fight the insidious lure of that message and realize its deception: No, it won't make things better; no, I won't have just one. He constantly has to remind himself, "I am an alcoholic and I cannot control my drinking. Part of my disease wants me to think that I can, but I know better, and I know, for the life I want to lead, I have to avoid using alcohol as an escape."

KEEP ON DETACHING

If your parent has taken steps to get sober but has been unable to make it stick, you're only too aware of how difficult dealing with a slip can be. Diane has shared the huge letdown she felt when her father resumed drinking. Such a reaction is only natural; after all, we've lived through so much suffering that sobriety means more than just about anything to us. It's everything we're hoping for, the only possible path to a healthy, happy home life. And then to have our parent spend some time sober only to relapse, well, it hits hard.

Because of the powerful feelings a slip can evoke, it's vital for us to maintain a healthy detachment as our parent is trying to get sober. Only with a detached perspective will we be able not to take the slip personally and not come down hard on our parent for failing. With our hopes raised by the alcoholic's new-found resolve to give up drinking, we can very easily get crushed by the disappointment and wind up spilling destructive reactions: "How could you do this when things were going so well?" "All your progress is right down the drain." "You're never going to stop." "You never really wanted to get sober." "You haven't changed; you still care more about drinking than you do about us."

Such reactions constitute a slip on *our* part, because they show we've lost sight of all that we've learned about handling the family disease. They are utterly destructive and have a frightening capability of ripping apart the alcoholic when he's already at his most vulnerable. As disappointing as a slip may be for us, we can't forget that it's infinitely worse for our parent. He's the one who couldn't make sobriety stick, after all. He feels like a total failure, like he's thrown whatever progress he has made right out the window. And he has a disease inside him that's saying: "Go ahead, have another drink. It's the best way out. You'll feel better. It doesn't matter now anyway. Don't you want to feel better?"

If we don't detach during a slip, we're bound to blurt out something that will greatly compound the guilt and suffering our parent is already experiencing. And such feelings will only make it harder for him to summon the strength to take another crack at sobriety. This is a time when we must show compassion and support, not reproach. We need to show him that we know how hard it is, and that he shouldn't judge himself so harshly just because he had a relapse. By adopting such an approach, we can help nourish his broken spirit and bolster his resolve and make it much easier for him to keep the small slip from growing into a bigger one.

THE PERILS OF OVERPROTECTING

As we gain a greater understanding of how hard it can be for an alcoholic to stay sober, our tendency is to try to make things easier for him. Often in cahoots with our non-drinking parent, we can conjure up all kinds of little ploys to protect him. We might warn other people not to serve him drinks. We might rip up the invitation to the neighborhood cocktail party. We might rig it so every trip out to eat winds up at a fast-food place where no liquor is served. Maybe somebody in the family will come down with a bug the day of the relative's wedding, where everyone knows the booze will be flowing. Or we might find some reason why someone in the family has to join him on his trip downtown (after all, if he goes alone, he might stop at the liquor store or a bar).

The list goes on and on. In fact, we could make a full-time job out of protecting him from situations where alcohol will be present, or from occasions or activities that we suspect might tempt him to drink, whether because of stress, peer pressure or because he always drank in that setting in the past. But the simple truth is that protecting the alcoholic during recovery is just as counter-productive as it is when he is drinking. While we certainly want to be supportive and encouraging, we must face the fact that it's the problem drinker's responsibility, not ours, to learn how to adjust to life without alcohol. By sneaking around and hatching schemes to protect him, we're only sending him a message—and we must know he's getting the message, no matter how subtle we think we are—that we don't think he can do it alone. Our lack of faith will hurt his feelings, add to his sense of inadequacy and raise serious questions in his mind about whether he can do it on his own. Much as with enabling, this is a case where our best intentions can actually aggravate the situation.

We have to let go of the urge to play the puppeteer, manipulating the strings of the alcoholic's world. Hard as it is, we have to let him stand on his own. And rather than taking actions that say to him we don't think he can do it, we should concentrate on showing him we have great faith in his ability to stay sober.

We also can't forget the importance of caring for ourselves. It's very easy, when we feel compelled to be the alcoholic's caretaker, to slip back into forgetting about progress in our lives. "I'm so worried about my mom that I feel like I can't do anything without thinking about how it will affect her sobriety," says Jeanine. "I'm afraid to go out with my friends because she might get lonely. One time she wanted to go out to eat but I had to study for a big test. She said she had been home all day and really needed to get out. I didn't want to go, but she kept pressuring me, and I was afraid if I didn't go that she might get so upset she'd want a drink. So I ended up going."

Jeanine's feelings are shared by virtually everyone who has ever dealt with an alcoholic during early sobriety. But we need to constantly remind ourselves that we cannot control the alcoholic's sobriety any more than we could control the drinking. When my mom was newly sober I wanted to make her life paradise. I wanted to protect her and fuss over her and soothe her troubles, and generally make things so blissful that she wouldn't dream of taking a drink. But such behavior is destructive. It's important to be considerate, even for us to go out of our way to offer a kind word and do nice things for our parent. But we must not make it our life's mission. Nobody can make someone else's life eternally happy. The alcoholic has to and will learn to deal with problems and trying moments just as all of us do. It's a part of the recovery process. If Jeanine needed to study for her test, she could take care of that part of her life in a way that didn't hurt her mother. "I really would like to go, but doing well on this exam is very important to me. Why don't we go tomorrow night?" Such a response is not likely to shatter the alcoholic. Not only can he handle more than we might think, he has to for recovery to be complete. Experts agree that one of the surest ways to bring on a relapse is by constantly doing things that give the alcoholic the idea that you're afraid that's what will happen. We need to detach, to have faith, and to show that faith—for our own benefit as well as for our parent's.

GUARDING AGAINST HIGH EXPECTATIONS

We often have a pre-determined notion of what life without drinking will be like. We might imagine peaceful evenings at home together, pleasant family outings or relaxing, orderly meals. But whatever our conception may be, we need to be careful about clinging to unrealistically high expectations during early sobriety.

The alcoholic, after all, is undergoing a tremendous adjustment. Indeed, so is the entire family. We have lived with alcoholism for so long, and the disease has worked its way into us so deeply, that we need to allow time for things to settle back into a comfortable and contented routine. The alcoholic may seem edgy and quick to anger. Sometimes he may even seem as confused or incoherent as when he was drinking, a condition often referred to as "dry drunk." Other times he may seem sullen or withdrawn, as though he wants nothing to do with you. To avoid disappointment, we need to maintain an awareness that recovery is a process and that years of alcohol abuse cannot be undone overnight.

In many cases, too, we might feel hurt or neglected because our newly sober parent is practically never at home. Maybe it's because he's attending A.A. meetings, or off spending time with the friends he has made at those meetings. Just try to understand that the meetings are not social occasions but your parent's lifeline to sobriety. Try not to take it personally in the sense that he would rather be with these virtual strangers than with you. He needs those people, who, having been down once themselves and having shared the horrors of the disease, can offer him strength and hope in a way that we simply cannot, no matter how devoted we are. Frequent attendance at A.A. meetings, in which alcoholics share their experiences and support one another in taking charge of their lives without alcohol, often can be the key to staying sober. A.A. itself, in fact, recommends that newcomers attend "90 meetings in 90 days" when they first enter the program.

AN INTERNAL CLOCK

There's no exact timetable for recovering from alcoholism. Some people may never leave their jobs (though this is quite rare), or they might get right back to work after leaving a rehabilitation center. Others may feel they cannot yet cope with the working world and not seek a job for a year or more. Some alcoholics may experience rapid progress in rebuilding themselves emotionally and psychologically and might seem to have achieved a contented sobriety within months of stopping drinking. Others can take years to get to the same place.

We need to be aware that the process takes varying amounts of time and be careful not to be judgmental if our parent isn't progressing the way we'd hoped. It's not his fault any more than the drinking was. Harboring an attitude that says, "When are you going to get it together already?" or "You're really not doing a very good job of adjusting"—will only make a hard struggle harder. The alcoholic is doing his best, and it isn't for us to set standards for him. It can be dangerously easy for us to watch over the alcoholic constantly, assessing his performance of sobriety day in, day out, as if we were making out his report card. We might nag him about not going to enough meetings, or about going to too many. We might not like his new friends, or disapprove of his keeping in touch with former drinking partners. But no matter what the issue, we have no right to sit in judgment of him. Indeed, this is a very common aspect of *our* disease; those of us who live with alcoholics tend to spend so many years hovering over them, spying on them, nagging them and scolding them that we often have a hard time letting go of this damaging judgmental attitude. As with the over-protective instinct, this will only betray our lack of faith in the alcoholic and increase his feelings of being inadequate. We want him to be an adult. We want him to take responsibility. The way to help him achieve that is not by treating him like a child.

LOOKING AT OURSELVES

Earlier we looked at how easy it is for us to become obsessed with our parent's drinking and to turn our entire lives into missions to stop it. We saw how futile and harmful that can be, not only because we're powerless over the drinking, but also because it stirs resentments in the alcoholic, heightens his feelings of worthlessness and fuels his self-pitying sense that everyone is picking on him.

It's equally easy to become obsessed with sobriety and again to focus all our attention on the alcoholic, watching him, judging him and clearing his path of any obstacles we think might cause a slip. It's helpful for us to see that such behavior is also futile and harmful. We can take a big step to rid ourselves of this tendency and make things better for everyone by paying attention to our own lives instead.

Feeling left out, perhaps, because your parent is always off at meetings? Why not find a meeting of your own to attend (Alateen would be a great idea, if you're not going already), or get involved in a new club or activity? Rather than fretting and fussing over your parent's shaky hold on sobriety, why not explore how a change in your attitude might make things easier for him? Not working to improve our own lives is, like the habit of judging the alcoholic, part of the diseased pattern that we fall into. And now is a good time to look at that and change it. Maybe, without even knowing it, you're displaying a lack of faith in your parent's ability to stay sober. Maybe you rush right home every day so you can keep him company when he sips his ginger ale. Maybe you pass up the weekend camping trip with friends because he might get lonely or need you for something. Maybe, if he suggests an activity, you feel 100 percent obligated to go along with it, no matter if you have prior plans or really want to do something else. We're talking about a question of degree here. It's great to be loyal and to let your parent know how much you care. That can give him a lot of strength through his transitional period. But the point is that we shouldn't do it to the extent that, in pushing our lives to the back seat, we impart to our parent a distinct sense that we have serious doubts about whether he can stay dry.

We've talked about how stagnation sets in during the active drinking. Life reels out of control and nothing seems to change, certainly not for the better. That's the way things proceed until we in the family can manage the courage and awareness to step away, let go of our grim, silent determination to do something about the drinking and start embracing the ideas that we've been looking at throughout the book. And as we've seen, the ensuing growth that we begin to experience can, by allowing the alcoholic to face the consequences of his drinking and by not adding to his huge feelings of guilt and inadequacy, play a key role in the alcoholic deciding to get help.

In the same way, perhaps the best way we can help the alcoholic during early sobriety is by helping ourselves. When we're active participants in our own lives, trying new things, establishing new friendships or building on those we have, we're naturally going to exude a positive, healthy attitude that surely will be noticed by those around us. We want to encourage and support our parent through this difficult time, but we also want to encourage and support ourselves. We are not our parent's keepers. We're only our own keepers, and the better job we do of it and the more we focus on our own growth, the greater positive influence we will bring to bear on the family as a whole. And that can do more good than we might ever suspect. It allows us to show support for our parent in just the right mix with faith in his ability to stay sober. It allows us to convey an understanding of what he's going through without interfering or over-protecting. And in showing strength and growth in rebuilding our own lives, it gives our parent belief and motivation in doing the same for himself.

A PARTING THOUGHT

We've talked a lot in this chapter about many of the difficult transitions that can be a part of your parent's pursuit of sobriety. We've looked at how we must guard against unrealistic expectations and how the recovery process can be a rocky road that can cause your parent to lose his way and slip. We've also seen how the struggle our parent is undergoing can sometimes make it feel as though things are barely better than when he was drinking.

Though it's important to recognize these potential pitfalls, we can't lose sight of the larger picture, which is that there is an enormous amount to be grateful for. Even if your parent is having slips and can't seem to make sobriety work, think about how great it is that he has faced the gravity of the problem and is trying to do something about it. Think about how hopeless things seemed and how hopeful they are now.

By far the biggest hurdle in dealing with the disease is having the alcoholic admit that he has no control over his drinking and that he must seek treatment before his life gets any worse. It can take years for some alcoholics to overcome that hurdle, and, sadly, some never do. So there's much gratitude in order, even for a sobriety that's coming in fits and starts. It's what we've always been holding out hope for amid our seemingly endless, wearying bouts of despair. It's a blessed sign that the alcoholic's once-impregnable denial is finally weakening, that there are stirrings of a realization that his only chance for a fulfilled life in the future is to leave the bottle in his past.

This is an immense realization for your parent to make. Let's count our blessings; a glint of light is twinkling where once there was only darkness.

Epilogue:
Changing What You Can

You may recall the story about how my father, in response to my worried inquiry as to when my mother's drinking problem might improve, flatly projected that all would be right in approximately six weeks. His so-certain projection gave me comfort and reassurance, though very temporarily; deep down I knew his timetable was nothing but wishful thinking. Disappointment and despair—more familiar feelings—came flooding back in no time.

For a long time I was convinced that the only way those feelings would ever be lifted was if my mother stopped drinking. I hitched my personal well-being entirely to the sobriety wagon. Many nights I fought sleep thinking that life could never even be tolerable until the dreaded bottle—how I hated the very sight of it—was out of the picture entirely. Because I wanted so desperately to have my "old" mother back and to have the dark cloud lifted from my life, I stubbornly clung to a futile conviction that I would find a way—some way, any way—to get her to stop. I would remind her of how warm and loving our lives together had been, and how they could be that way again. I would take care of her and look after her, enabling her in a hundred ways, certain that with enough support and compassion I could "love" the drinking right out the door. Other times, frustration and hopelessness mounting with each failed attempt at control, I would try to "punish" it out of her; if she can see clearly how much agony I'm in, I reasoned, she'll feel so awful she'll have no choice but to stop.

Such were my understandable but misguided approaches to alcoholism. I learned the hard way that we have no power over another person's compulsion to drink. It was a frightening realization at first. I fought it. I was sure I just hadn't come up with the right strategy yet. I hated to think I could not make one iota of difference. But finally there was no getting around it: The disease was a lot bigger and more powerful than I was.

Initially this fact hit like a punch in the nose. I resigned myself to it. I accepted it very grudgingly. But with the help and support of Alateen and later Al-Anon, and by sharing my experiences and feelings with others who have lived with the problem, I came to view this new knowledge in an entirely different light. I realized that a sure path to frustration is tying our life's outlook to something that's beyond our control. And I realized that by accepting alcoholism as a disease that I was powerless over, I could let go of my grim determination to do something about it, and instead shift my sights to things I *could* do something about.

For those of us who live or have lived with an alcoholic parent, this is the beginning of recovery. It's also the core of all we've been talking about in this book.

Probably it's as hard for you as it was for me to accept your powerlessness over the disease. You may have even picked up this book because you thought it would help you find a way to stop your parent from drinking; at the beginning I went to Alateen meetings for precisely that reason myself. But I hope, after giving thought to the ideas we've been discussing, that you've come to see that letting go of efforts to control the drinking can be the starting point to a whole new—and infinitely healthier—way of living.

Suppose there's a glass of water on a table. It's an eight-ounce glass with four ounces of liquid. Is it half-empty or half-full? The answer can say a lot about our outlook on life: The pessimist focuses on how much is missing. The optimist likes to think of how much there is.

We have a similar choice to make in the way we deal with our parent's alcoholism. We can dwell on the negative side—that nothing we do can rid him of the disease—or we can look at the positive—that there's a lot we can do to make our lives better and to lessen the impact of the drinking on us. Count this book and its author staunchly in the optimist camp.

Is this naive optimism, thinking that we can improve our lives and do so even if our parent is still drinking? Far from it. It's a realistic, healthy and very attainable goal—one that I was able to achieve, that thousands of other kids from alcoholic homes have achieved, and one that you can achieve as well.

The tools we can use to build ourselves a better life are the substance of the foregoing pages. They're right before you, ready to be used, and the great thing is, you don't have to be a master craftsman to benefit from them. We give them an honest effort and they work; they lift our spirits and make our lives more manageable. We have no guarantee that our parent will find sobriety. But we do have a guarantee, a rock-solid one, that we can change our attitudes and shift our focus and do positive things for ourselves nonetheless. And that holds true no matter how much we love the alcoholic and how bad his disease may become.

For a long time I felt I had no choice but to feel bad. But putting the tools to work shows that we do have a choice. We begin to realize that we don't have to feel hurt and humiliated when our alcoholic parent insults us; we can understand that he has a disease that has filled him with poison and that drives him to vent his frustrations on those closest to him. We realize that we don't have to take his neglect, disinterest or meanness to heart, because these, too, are symptoms of his sickness. We realize that we didn't cause the disease and that we have no ability to control it or cure it. We realize that we can hate the disease and yet go right on loving the parent who has it. And we realize that in detaching ourselves in this manner, in limiting the disease's ability to inflict pain and warp our thinking, we allow ourselves to let go of our behavior—the protecting and the rescuing that only insulate the alcoholic from the destruction his drinking is doing and the blaming and punishing that only make him feel more hopeless and worthless—which has the unintended effect of making the problem worse.

Life can be better, starting right now. The tools are yours. Pick them up and put them to work. And as you do, remember that there are millions of others of us who, in spirit anyway, are working right alongside you.

Appendix A
Dealing with a Crisis

As we know from our discussion of alcoholism's progression, the untreated disease only gets worse. The problem drinker steadily loses any ability to control his drinking, and the result of this unhappy process frequently is that what once were problems now become full-fledged crises. Where once it was the neighbors who complained about noise, now it's the police who are showing up on your doorstep. Maybe the alcoholic used to fall and suffer minor bruises and bumps; now he may be in the hospital, suffering from the far more serious consequences of an automobile accident or barroom brawl. The sad truth is that crises are not uncommon in alcoholic homes. As the drinking worsens, so do the problems it provokes, and it's not uncommon for the situation suddenly to involve not only police and hospitals, but also social workers, mental institutions, bill collectors and credit bureaus, as well as friends, neighbors and other family members. So you're not alone if these or any other ugly events are occurring in your home.

That may make you feel somewhat relieved. But what do you do if a crisis is looming—or already under way—at home? If you or someone else is being physically abused? If the alcoholic can barely stand up, yet is adamant about driving the family somewhere as planned? If you fear the alcoholic has (whether intentionally or not) taken an overdose of pills?

A thorough discussion of handling crises brought on by alcoholism would require another book and is not within the scope of our discussion here. What we're offering instead is a thumbnail guide to some of the most difficclt situations you will ever have to face—a basic overview of what to do when things get really bad.

BREAK THE SILENCE

The first thing to keep in mind is that you have a right—indeed, a responsibility—to look out for your own physical and mental well-being. (If you have younger brothers and sisters, the responsibility extends to them as well.) Absolutely no good can come from leaving yourself in a situation where you're at high risk for harm. But it can be very hard for us to see this clearly when we're in the throes of a crisis. The isolation we've talked so much about makes us want to hide or withdraw—certainly not to divulge any of the horrible goings-on to someone else. It's as though the disease imposes a gag order on the family: Thou shalt not talk about the drinking. Thou shalt not seek help. One of the most wicked things about this disease is the way it encourages, even urges, its victims to keep silent about it.

But this is a message we must fight. Absolutely the worst thing to do in a crisis is to go it alone, to try to hide from it or hope it blows over. DO NOT SUFFER IN SILENCE! If things are beginning to get out of hand, or if you or another family member already has been sexually abused or is in physical danger, get in touch immediately with someone in the extended family: perhaps an aunt or uncle, a grandparent, a cousin, even a trusted adult friend—any adult who might be able to offer help. (As we've seen, often the sober parent is so preoccupied and confused with the drinking—or is trying to hide from it herself—that she cannot see the situation clearly enough to help.) Whoever you reach, tell him exactly what you're feeling and what's going on. "Dad's drunk again and he's running around the house breaking things. I'm really afraid." Or, "Mom hit me last night and told me she would do it again if I ever said anything to anyone." "Dad just passed out and I think he took a lot of pills. What should I do?" Often the person you speak to may help by coming right over and physically removing you from the situation. Or, if that's not possible or not necessary, he may call for medical help.

Sometimes you may not be able to reach a concerned family member. Or maybe nobody lives near enough to be of immediate help. When this is the case and things are at or near the crisis stage, you may have no choice but to call the police. This can be a very difficult and painful step to take. You'll probably feel embarrassed and ashamed if you do need to call them, and you may also feel guilty about airing the family's dirty laundry. These feelings are entirely understandable, *but you mustn't let them sidetrack you from making that call*. Sometimes your call may even result in still another terrible occurrence, such as your parent being taken to jail or to a mental institution, traumatic consequences that might infuriate your drinking parent and make you feel almost hopelessly guilty and disloyal. BUT YOU ARE DOING THE RIGHT THING WHEN YOU REACH OUT FOR HELP. Loyalty has nothing to do with it. If your parent thinks you've betrayed him, that's too bad. That's part of his disease—and his irrational, alcoholic thinking. His reaction—anger, scorn, whatever it may be—isn't going to make you feel any better about your actions. But the fact is, you did what you had to do. Your first loyalty must be to yourself. Your well-being must be your top priority. If the alcoholic perceives your looking out for yourself as disloyalty, well, you're just going to have to live with it, and keep reminding yourself that it's not an issue of loyalty at all. It's an issue of self-preservation.

MOVE NOW, THINK LATER

It is definitely not normal—or legal—for your parent to beat or physically abuse you in any way. The same holds true for any attempts by your parent to fondle, caress or engage in any kinds of sexual contact with you. You must take whatever measure is necessary to stop the abuse immediately. If you are being abused, or you have been in the past and are in danger of it again, do not stop to make your phone calls in the house. LEAVE YOUR HOME IMMEDIATELY. Whoever you need to call, do it from a phone booth or from a neighbor's house. Your immediate physical safety is always the first thing you must look out for. When in doubt, remove yourself from the threatening situation and take it from there. It's an old cliche, but it's very true: better to be safe than sorry. But once you are safe, be sure to alert someone to the situation. Call a family member. Call your doctor. Call a child- or sexual-abuse hotline, whose number you can get from the information operator or the phone book. But call somebody. Do not keep it a secret; in the long run that's the worst thing you can do. Bottling it up only increases your already immense mental and emotional burden, and only increases the likelihood of the abuse continuing. Talking about it is very hard, and you may feel an urge to protect your parent and not supply all the details of the true extent of the abuse. But you must protect yourself first and foremost; you're being victimized, and when you talk to adult family members, counselors or the police, it's important that you tell the whole story. It's for your own good, and in the long run, for your parent's own good, too.

There is a whole network of trained professionals out there who want to help you. They understand the trauma you're undergoing, can help you through the immediate crisis, and will keep your case confidential. Take advantage of these resources. It's your right—and your responsibility to yourself.

DANGER BEHIND THE WHEEL

A drunk driving a car is a disaster waiting to happen. As a general rule, do whatever you possibly can to avoid riding with a driver who is intoxicated. Nothing less than your life may be at stake. Maybe a potential tragedy can be avoided if you suggest that someone else—your other parent, an older brother or sister, a grandparent, etc.—drive. If the drinker resists giving up the keys, you might try telling it to him straight: "I'm afraid because I don't think you're in a condition to drive." If nobody else can drive, or if your drinking parent is adamant about driving, then it's time for serious action. Trust your instincts; if they tell you that your parent is in no shape to drive, do not get in the car. Stick to your guns even if the alcoholic insists he is fine and that he's perfectly capable of driving. Problem drinkers almost always think they're fine; their distortion of their ability to function is just another aspect of their denial.

Sometimes you may not have any choice but to go along. Your parent may threaten you or physically force you into the car. But do whatever you can to avoid things getting to that point. Try to think of ways around the problem. Can you or the family stay over—or at least put off the travel plans until the drinker sobers up? If not, are there other ways to get where you're going? Train, bus, taxi?

Taking any of these measures—refusing to ride with your parent, calling a taxi, etc.—requires considerable courage. Your parent will probably be angry at you. He'll accuse you of overreacting. He'll insist that you obey him. But again, your first priority must always be your own physical well-being. If riding with the drinker is not safe, do whatever you must to avoid getting in the car.

THE THREAT OF FIRE

Many fires are started by problem drinkers who fall asleep or who are careless with cigarettes, matches, candles or stoves. We cannot keep a 24-hour vigil over the alcoholic, so it's not possible to be absolutely sure he never leaves a burner on or falls asleep with a cigarette in his hand. The best we can do is be prepared in the event that there is a fire. Make sure you know the location of the escape routes from your home, be it an outside staircase, a window that leads to the roof, or whatever. Whatever your route, remove yourself from the home as quickly as possible. Do not rush around to alert other family members; that is almost always a fatal error. Shout a warning at the top of your lungs, but get out of the house right away. Call the fire department only once you're safely away from the scene.

CONTACTS

There's no telling what might happen when our parent's drinking problem becomes progressively worse. We can do ourselves a big favor, however, by being prepared for the most basic emergencies. Keep a list of names and numbers of people and sources to contact in the event of a crisis: family members; the police; the fire department; the hospital; hotlines for poison, drugs, alcohol, child abuse and sexual abuse (you can get the numbers from the white pages or the community/government pages of your phone book); your family doctor and/or clergyman; a counselor you or the family may have worked with; even a trusted friend or neighbor. Carry the list with you at all times.

Chances are you'll never have to consult it. But it is much better to be prepared. Taking even the most basic actions is very difficult under the stress of a family crisis. You're taking a significant and positive step to ensure your well-being by knowing who to contact and how to reach them before the trouble actually hits.

Appendix B
Where to Go for Help

There are a number of sources of help and information for young people living with an alcoholic parent. Topping the list is Alateen, a worldwide support group of young people who, like us, live or have lived with someone (almost always a parent) with a drinking problem. Held regularly in hundreds of communities throughout the country, Alateen meetings have helped hundreds of thousands of young people cope with their parent's drinking by offering strength, support and loving guidance on any and every concern or problem that may arise.

To locate an Alateen group in your area, check the white pages of your phone book under Al-Anon or Al-Anon Information Service; the people at Al-Anon will have the information you need on Alateen. You also can obtain some very helpful pamphlets and other reading material by writing to:

Al-Anon Family Group Headquarters
P.O. Box 182
Madison Square Station
New York, NY 10159

Be sure to specify that you want material pertaining to Alateen.

For further information on alcoholism-related services in your area, look in the Yellow Pages under "Alcoholism" or call your town or city department of public health and ask where you might go for guidance and information. If that doesn't work, try looking in the Yellow Pages under various related headings: "Social Workers"; "Social Service Organizations"; "Therapists"; or "Counselors." There's a wealth of information in the phone book; by making a few calls and asking some questions you can almost always find someone who will listen to you, offer suggestions and provide relevant information.

Additional reading materials on the problems of living with an alcoholic are available from:

National Council on Alcoholism
12 West 21st Street
New York, NY 10010
(212) 206-6770

and

National Clearinghouse for Alcohol Information
Box 2345
Rockville, MD 20852

INDEX

Addiction, 3, 5, 8, 96, 98
Al-Anon, 30, 80, 112, 121
Alateen, 29-30, 35, 42, 75, 80, 81, 107, 112, 121
Alcohol rehabilitation centers, 87, 96, 97, 106
Alcoholics, 3-5, 61, 86; admission of disease, 60, 65, 68, 92-93, 109; as children, 44-46, 61, 68, 73-74; decision to stop drinking, 19, 93, 95; defined, 2; facing reality, 19, 61, 65, 69, 71-81, 83, 87, 91, 95, 108; inability to control drinking, 3, 11, 12, 13, 16, 39-40, 42-43, 63, 99, 101-2, 115; justification for drinking, 6, 14-15, 49, 50, 66-68, 69, 92; loving support for, 83-93; not wilfully hurting others, 12, 39-40, 46; responsibility to learn to live without alcohol, 74, 104-5, 107, 109; treatment of, 60-69; use of alcohol to escape psychological pain, 7-8, 75-76, 97, 102
Alcoholics Anonymous (A.A.), 91, 99, 100, 101, 106
Alcoholism, 1-9, 42; causes of, 8; effects of, 102, 22-24, 31-32, 44, 46, 51, 79; as family disease, 21-35, 48, 51, 54, 56-57, 58, 92, 105, 107; intensified by enabling, 75-76; not moral failing, 13; physical, emotional, and psychological disease, 101 (see also Disease concept of alcoholism); predisposition to, 8, 21; progression, 2-3, 5, 8, 24, 100, 115; symptoms of, 4-5; treatment of, 95, 96-99; victims of, 52
American Medical Association, 11
Anger, 48, 63; alcoholic parent, 6, 60, 86, 91; children, 26, 39, 45, 55-56, 62
Antabuse, 97-98
Attitude(s), 2, 18-19, 22, 30, 42-43, 48, 108, 113; judgmental, 107; and sobriety, 97, 98

Blackmail, 45, 77-78
Blackouts, 5
Blaming, 13, 19, 60, 64-66, 69, 86, 87 91, 92, 114; letting go of, 88-39

Child: parent as, 44-46, 61, 68, 73-74
Children of alcoholics, xi, xii, xv, 1-2; and cause, control, cure, 11-19, 24, 26, 35, 37, 43, 59, 63, 64, 68, 104-5, 111-14; helping during sobriety, 108-9; likelihood of becoming alcoholic, 8, 21; and rescue of sober parent, 54-55; responsibility for own lives, needs, 33-35, 41-42, 45-46, 79, 80-81, 104, 107-9, 113-14, 116-17, 118, 119
Compassion, 91, 92, 103, 112
Compulsion to drink, 2-3, 8, 11, 16, 19, 39-40, 45, 69, 85, 97, 112; halting, 98-99
Concentration, difficulty with, 23-24
Confrontation, 7, 74, 85-87, 88
Coping behavior, 8, 31, 97, 101
Counselor(s), 79, 80, 87, 118, 120
Crisis situations, 79-80, 115-20
Cure, 18-19, 98

Denial: by alcoholic parent, 6-7, 9, 14, 19, 60, 61, 65, 66, 75, 99-100, 110, 119; alcoholism as disease of, xiii, 6-7; by family, 27, 29, 57; by sober parent, 49-51
Detachment, 35, 37-46, 63-64, 83, 90-91; in confrontation, 87, 88; from hurts, 66; with love, 84-85; from sober parent, 58; with sobriety, 89, 102-3, 105
Detoxification, 96-97